A Woman of the Century

Frances Minerva Nunnery *(1898–1997)*

A Woman of the Century

Frances Minerva Nunnery *(1898–1997)*

Her Story in Her Own Memorable Voice as Told to Cecil Dawkins

Edited by Cecil Dawkins

With a Foreword by Max Evans

UNIVERSITY OF NEW MEXICO PRESS
ALBUQUERQUE

Library of Congress Cataloging-in-Publication Data

Nunnery, Frances Minerva, 1898-1997.
   A woman of the century, Frances Minerva Nunnery (1898-1997)
   : her story in her own memorable voice as told to Cecil
   Dawkins / edited by Cecil Dawkins.— 1st ed.
p. cm.
ISBN 0-8263-2851-2 (alk. paper)
   1. Nunnery, Frances Minerva, 1898-1997.   2. Women ranchers—New Mexico—Biography.   3. Ranch life—New Mexico.
   4. New Mexico—Biography.   I. Dawkins, Cecil, 1927– II. Title.
CT275.N7866 A3 2002
978.9'05'092—dc21

                    2002006442

❙ CONTENTS ❙

No! Frances Martin, the name by which I knew Frances Nunnery when I lived in Taos, does not fit into the category of "They don't make them like that any more." They never did—not in the 2000s, the 1900s, or any other century. A lot of great women have lived in the West, and I knew personally some of those who were born here in New Mexico or came and stayed to contribute mightily. I was acquainted with Mabel Dodge Luhan, the Taos arts doyenne; Fern Sawyer, the Hall of Fame cowgirl; Mildred Clark (Madame Millie) Cusey; and countless others who remain mostly unknown. Frances was not like any of them. She was unique.

We are so very lucky that Cecil Dawkins met Frances in the late 1960s when Frances was a highly successful Taos realtor. The resulting friendship led to this wonderful portrait of Frances's courage, skill, and wit, almost beyond belief except to those who knew her. We who had the privilege of knowing Frances will recognize that in telling her story to Cecil Dawkins she often downplayed her splendiferous achievements.

We can now share the ninety-nine-year journey of her adventurous life, from her birth in Covington, Kentucky, to her childhood on a Virginia tobacco farm, to her first bad marriage with a man thrust on her by her mother and her successful getaway from him in Colorado, and on to Albuquerque with a nine-month-old baby. There she fought her way into prominence and profit in assorted businesses. One of them eventually led to the founding of the giant UPS—United Parcel Service.

Frances became a successful rancher and later an entrepreneur in the Magdalena/Datil area. Her down-home, down-in-the-mud, up-on-the-mountain experiences with cattle, horses, hogs, and all the wild and domesticated animals it takes to survive in a harsh and lonely environment are as educational as they are soul building to those readers who admire pure spunk and natural wit and wisdom.

Find how Frances "does in" a persistently challenging neighbor-rancher who, taking advantage of her gender and generosity, started out stealing her grass and moved on to stealing her animals.

See Frances as a deputy sheriff when she handles a deadly situation with great finesse.

Join in and root for her as she rebuilds and runs the Navajo Lodge in Datil and turns it into a nightclub where she does her own singing for the enthusiastic customers.

Ride with her as she drives heavy rigs hauling cattle for ranchers over great and dangerous distances, accepting it all with good humor.

Frances Nunnery Martin's story is one to be savored. It has been said that she seldom shared her inner feelings, but this strong woman didn't need to: her actions told everything. They were there for all to see and to absorb in awe. She was a woman to relish. You will find much more in her story than I can describe in this foreword. Read her story and tell your closest friends. You will have done them a special favor.

Max Evans

Albuquerque, New Mexico
Author of *Madame Millie, Bluefeather Fellini, The Hi Lo Country,* and *The Rounders.*

When Frances Minerva Nunnery was born in 1898 the Wright brothers had yet to launch their first airplane, years would pass before homes had telephones and radios, and families still took their Sunday afternoon drives by horse and buggy. People were known to travel miles to see the newfangled horseless carriage that had just made its appearance. Yet Frances would live to see autos and airplanes and radios and telephones and televisions commonplace in America, and to witness men in space suits tripping lightly across the surface of the moon.

Frances's earliest memory was of being taken to see the funeral train, all draped in black, of the assassinated president, William McKinley, as it passed through Pittsburgh in 1901. She was three years old. It was an experience she remembered to her death "as if it were yesterday." Yet she would live through two World Wars, the "police action" in Korea, the folly of Vietnam, and the assassination of another president, John F. Kennedy.

But Frances's autobiography does not concern itself with the great events of history. It is the story of a self-sufficient little girl hauling water and working in the fields pinching suckers from the fragile new plants on a Kentucky tobacco farm; of a youngster who, when she got a "licking," never cried but "stood there as a matter of pride" and took her medicine, and of a thirteen-year-old joining the labor force at the H. J. Heinz plant in Pittsburgh where she saw all these dressed-up "ladies beating on typewriters." Her story takes us through her marriage at twenty-one to a man she didn't know or love, through childbirth and, finally, in the Model T she'd bought with one of her last Liberty Bonds from World War I and converted into her first camper, running away from a hateful marriage and striking out for New Mexico. It was the spring of 1921.

Her memoir takes us through enterprising early adventures in Albuquerque, the market crash of 1929, running two big ranches in Catron County with the help of her children and a hired man, and rebuilding the Navajo Lodge in Datil where she was proprietor, chief cook and bottle washer, and entertainer. Eventually she became a deputy sheriff and, finally, lived in every part of New Mexico. In her later years in Taos she knew Mabel Dodge Lujan and Georgia O'Keeffe and other luminaries of New Mexico, the state she loved because, she said, "New Mexico has everything." In her seventies, out-of-town visitors to her home included actors Marlon Brando, Maureen Stapleton, and Kim Stanley.

At eighty-seven, suffering from arthritis ("And what's all this about 'minor arthritis pain'?" she wanted to know, "There's nothing minor about it. It's major."), Frances moved to Silver City in search of a warmer climate. Silver, as she called it, felt like home. The southern part of the state was familiar from her days driving semis at the end of World War II and, earlier, driving cattle from her ranches—Spur Ranch and Centerfire—down the Magdalena Driveway to the rail-head with the help of her daughter, her stepdaughter, and a couple of Spanish caballeros.

From her chair by the fireplace in her Silver City home, she tells the story of an amazing life that spanned the most astounding time in human history: the twentieth century. Taped when she was in her nineties, her autobiography is the personal story of a New Mexico woman's life and times told in her own voice rich with the humor and no-nonsense practicality of a woman who was not only a survivor but a winner on every stage life placed her.

In her last years Frances claimed to be in a race with George Burns to see who could live to be a hundred, a race, she said, in which the winner came in last. But Frances was a woman used to being first in just about everything. She lost the race by beating George to the finish line. She died in Silver City in 1997. She was ninety-nine years old.

—Cecil Dawkins, Santa Fe, fall 2001

❙ ACKNOWLEDGMENTS ❙

First of all, for the treasure that became this book I'm indebted to Frances herself, a woman whose schooling stopped after the third grade but whose learning and accomplishments continued till the end of her remarkable life.

In addition I am grateful to Janice Mars, without whose loyalty and help Frances would not have been able, at age ninety-two and almost blind, to record the six tapes telling me her life story. I also thank Janice for her invaluable encouragement throughout this project.

For help with clarifying details from days on the ranch my gratitude to Frances's stepdaughters Dorothy Major and Darlene Hall.

I am grateful to Frances's granddaughter Sara Peck and stepdaughter Dorothy Major for supplying photographs of Frances's early days in Albuquerque and on the ranch, and to Janice Mars and Sally Whiteley for later photographs, particularly from Frances's life in Taos.

I came to know that just about everybody in Northern New Mexico knew Frances, but I only met her when, after spending the summer of 1969 in Taos and realizing how much I hated to leave, I walked into the first real estate office I came to—a store front just off Taos plaza with a few animal skulls and Indian pots in the windows. The sign over the door said Northern New Mexico Real Estate Exchange. Reared back in her swivel chair with her feet in cowboy boots up on the desk sat a woman with arresting blue eyes in a face like the map of some mountain terrain, lines and tributaries branching off in all directions. She wore a beret I came to know as standard headgear subduing her fine silver hair, a flashy turquoise-and-silver watchband on her wrist, and a saucer-size turquoise-and-silver buckle on her belt. Frances that day was one month shy of her seventy-first birthday.

Those eyes were assessing me, waiting for me to speak up. I said I wanted to look at land. That morning Frances showed me eleven acres in Des Montes with views of the Truchas peaks to the south, Taos Mountain to the east, and to the west the sage desert with the Rio Grande Gorge streaking through. A crumbling ruin backed by cottonwoods and an old orchard with pear, apple, apricot, and green gage plum trees squatted between two irrigation ditches. We walked the length of the acreage and back, Frances in her cowboy boots, her back as straight as an aspen. I was ready to buy the place then and there, but the owner was out of town and I had to leave Taos the next morning.

But driving cross-country I kept seeing that ruin and those spectacular views. When I returned to Taos the following May the land was still for sale and I bought it. People told me to bulldoze the ruin out of the way, but Frances said I could save part of it. So I began shoveling off the sod roof to get to the vigas. In goggles, with a bandanna over my mouth, I took a sledge hammer to the rotted bricks on top of the walls till I came to adobe as hard as concrete, then began building my adobe house.

When business brought her out my way, Frances stopped by to see how the project was coming along. One day she asked if I liked to fish. I said I did. She told me to meet her at her place the next morning at five A.M. Fishing was Frances's passion. She liked getting an early start.

She had packed—I learned she always did—a picnic lunch of barbecued ribs and potato salad. Toward the end of this book she tells of getting to know writers and artists from the Wurlitzer Foundation. I'm sure some were along on that first outing to Hopewell Lake. Several, like me, bought land through Frances and settled in Taos. We fished all day, ate ribs and potato salad and, as Frances had a clear blues voice and liked to sing, we sang all the way home.

Frances loved cars. She'd had a Cadillac convertible in her sixties. When I knew her she owned three vehicles—a Ford Bronco for business and the mountains, a VW camper for the fishing trips, and a Thunderbird convertible, robin's-egg blue with a white top, for meeting prospective clients at the Albuquerque airport. It was hard for Frances to give up a prized possession. She kept that T Bird for years after she could no longer drive and you could no longer buy the leaded regular gas it took. She finally sold it in her nineties when, she said, she and the T Bird were both classics.

She was also well into her nineties when she gave me all her fishing gear because, she said, "I guess I won't be fishing any more." Her last fishing trip was already ten years in the past when one afternoon, unable to stand for any length of time, she'd set herself down in a lawn chair with its feet and her own in the shallow water of a lake near Silver City and baited and cast as expertly as always.

When I went to town for provisions I often stopped by Frances's office and found her sitting at her window with her feet up on her desk and her little ginger-colored toy poodles Rita Bird and Poupe Dulcie in her lap. During these years I heard Frances's life story in installments. I learned she'd been blues singer, rancher, roadhouse proprietor, deputy sheriff, and big-rig driver during World War II before settling in Taos.

Animals brought out a tenderness in Frances that she otherwise preferred to hide. On one all-day fishing expedition she was sitting on a lake bank with her fishing rod when something tipped her hat over her face. It turned out to be an abandoned puppy. She took it home, named it Girlie, and gave it a long, happy life. She saved an elkhound puppy she found in a Taos hotel lobby hemorrhaging from a botched spaying. She called it Elkie and nursed it back to health. Once, stopping by her house during a downpour, I found her grumbling about the stupidity of ducks while ministering gently to several yellow puff-ball babies who had nearly drowned in the rain, wrapping them in a towel and putting them in the oven with the door open and the heat on low. Soon they were up and running around the floor. One character in the novel I was writing the summer I met Frances was a savvy little mule. When the little mule died early in the story, Frances put down the book and never picked it up again.

At the age of seventy-seven, to escape Taos winters she moved to Williamsburg, New Mexico, and later to Silver City. I visited her in Silver City each fall and spring until her death in 1997 at age ninety-nine. In 1991, when I was leaving for a semester's teaching at the University of Hawaii, she asked me to send her letters on tape because her eyesight was failing. I agreed to if, in return, she would send me her life story. I'd heard it through the years, but I wanted it on tape in Frances's memorable voice. We struck the bargain. With the help of her friend Janice Mars, and with lots of laughter and frequent battles with both "this infernal machine" and Janice, Frances made the six sixty-minute tapes that became this memoir. She was ninety-two, still interested in everything, her mind sharp and active as it was till she died.

As a member of the Actor's Studio in New York City, Janice had become friends with actors Marlon Brando and Maureen Stapleton, and they've remained friends ever since. Also a singer, she had her own nightclub there, frequented by theatrical people like Lauren Bacall, Jason Robards and other luminaries. In 1972 she came to Taos to meet Frank Waters, whose books she admired. Affected profoundly by the Taos landscape, she decided to acquire land, and Frank Waters took her to meet Frances. The resulting friendship lasted for the rest of Frances's life. Janice, with another trusted friend, Rosa Acuna, was with her in the hospital when she died.

As the tapes were also letters to me, Frances began each one by responding to my last tape and telling news of her day: she'd made a strawberry pie that was "too runny," there'd been a little snow and it was still "sticking around," a friend had sent her an amaryllis and it had six blossoms, she'd send me a picture. Frances told her story as it came to her, with very little respect for chronology, sometimes rushing through a summary of years, then going back as it suited her to fill in the blanks. Editing the tapes took much splicing to keep the chronology straight, and where necessary for the sake of clarity I've provided details from the many times I heard her story piecemeal. The voice of the memoir is strictly Frances, her story as I'd always heard it, except, perhaps, she cleaned up her act a little: her favorite cuss—"What the goddamn hell!"—appears nowhere in these pages. Maybe she still heard her mother's voice telling her she ought to be more "respectable," by which Amelia Jane no doubt meant more conventionally ladylike, advice Frances rarely honored in her life.

A 1988 sketch of Frances appearing in *Taos Magazine* records that "A heavy-set prowler with robbery and rape in mind broke into Frances's house searching for a victim. Encountering the lady of the house, he raised a hand to attack. That was the last thing he remembered before he awoke to find himself trussed up like a turkey ready for basting, sitting in an ice-cold lake with a very large lump on his head. 'He needed a little cooling off, so I obliged him,' said Frances. She's never believed in wasting time or mincing words. The subject of the prowler was closed." This episode happened in Taos at her place on Lower Ranchitos Road, where she had drained a marsh and built two fishing ponds right outside her door. The author of the sketch was Tricia Hurst, whose humorous articles Frances enjoyed and whose daughter was Frances's godchild.

Nothing made Frances madder than to hear the tale about her cattle rustling during the Depression. "That's a damn lie and a tall tale," Hurst's article quotes her as saying, "and I'd like to see anyone prove it. As a matter of fact, I'll offer a reward. The only cattle I ever swiped were my own. You might say I re-rustled them after they'd been *borrowed* in the first place."

Hurst writes that during Frances's years as a deputy sheriff she claimed to hold many a marriage together. "I kind of ran interference when a couple were having their little spats and the husband was drunk out of his mind and his spouse was after him with a meat cleaver. I like to think I saved them a tidy sum in legal fees and burial services."

Frances always kept her eye out for good acreage. She dreamed of going to Alaska, a trip she had planned for her seventieth birthday but never made. "There's a section up there next to Siberia that would have made pretty good pickins—like the old days in New Mexico," Frances says in Hurst's article: "People kept telling me I'd be asking for trouble, because that's where the Russians are fiddling around. But what the devil does anyone think they would have done to a poor woman like me? Anyway, I'd have put on my old badge and toted along my .38 just to show them I wasn't about to put up with any tomfoolery.

A lady can never be too careful—great-grandmother or no great-grandmother." Hurst claimed it's been said that "any earth the federal government didn't own in New Mexico, Frances did."

Frank Waters wrote about "maverick" Frances in *Of Time and Change* (Denver: MacMurray & Beck, 1998), "She was for years the only land broker in the area . . . dealing only in ranches, great expanses of grazing land, and stands of timber. Much of the land lay in former Spanish and Mexican land grants whose titles were obscure or had been contested since American occupancy of the territory of New Mexico. Frances's work required a thorough knowledge of history, legal ramifications, and water and mineral rights. This paperwork research she conducted in a small combination office, kitchen, and bedroom in an old adobe building on a side street off the plaza. It was backed by her intimate knowledge of the land itself. Driving . . . across plains and mountains, she knew every watercourse, could tell at a glance that a stretch of grass was overgrazed, estimate the board feet and worth of a stand of timber. Tanned and weathered, she looked like a storied Earth Mother." She was "always in close touch with all the ranchers, cowboys, and workmen who often depended upon her advice. . . . When Taos expanded and changed into a tourist resort, she retired . . . to a secluded house and garden in southern New Mexico, where I still occasionally see her."

Frances liked jokes. Sometimes, to keep her mind sharp as she grew old, she made up her own. When she could no longer see well enough to read, friends sent pages of jokes to be read to her. When I visited, I was the reader. I'd have to wait at the end of every joke till Frances finished laughing. And she liked good talk. On my visits we spent our time talking in front of the fire. She often told me new tales of the old days. Earlier the stories had been over a drink, but by this time Frances had given up her bourbon.

Always practical, she's quoted by Hurst: "You can have your fancy cars, houses, jewelry, and all the rest . . . but you can't plant beans or corn on or in them, or run your cattle over them." An avid gardener, she never planted flowers, only, as she said, "what you can eat."

A *Taos News* photograph of her in her eighties shows her sitting on a stool picking vegetables in her quarter-acre garden irrigated with rainwater from her roof and held in a cistern of her own design. A few days before her eightieth birthday, *Taos News* writer Janice Daigh quoted her saying "with her irrefutable logic 'The Lord made the good dirt and gave me a shovel to dig it with. Why shouldn't I have a good garden?'"

In her nineties Frances still liked to dip into real estate, buying a house now and then, fixing it up and selling it. On my visits she sometimes sent me to check out a couple of houses for her. One I remember well: I came back and strongly advised against it. She asked lots of questions, I drove her past the house, and in spite of all I could say, she bought it because she liked the lot—it had fruit trees. She had it fixed up and sold it at a small profit, then held the paper for a buyer unable to qualify for a conventional mortgage. As she says in the memoir, she only wanted a little profit, not too much, so the new owner could make a little profit, too.

She thought her artist and writer friends were an impractical lot and did her best to keep us solvent. I never undertook anything of a practical nature without first passing it by Frances. She liked hearing all the details, and she always asked questions and gave sound advice. She never talked about all the ways she had helped people she knew and liked, but I learned she'd put a friend's daughter through the University of New Mexico, financed an inn up in the Taos ski valley for a chef looking to expand his horizons and when younger cooked many a casserole for acquaintances laid up with chronic illnesses. In her nineties she told visitors, "I can't cook for you any more, you'll have to look after yourself." Her freezer was always stocked with shrimp and steaks, and she liked to send out for her favorite Mexican dinner: cheese enchiladas.

Frances drew people to her because she was that rarity, a woman who—in times difficult for an independent woman—knew who she was and never became conventional. She probably made some enemies for the same reason.

Commenting about the Hurst article on Frances and other Taos octogenarians, a *Taos News* writer said, "Frances stood apart from the others, who appeared to revel in outrageous statements, one-liner aphorisms that accented their ... anti-establishment stance as members of a geriatric counterculture. By contrast, she speaks in understated nuggets of common sense. She considers her unusual experiences as obvious ways of coping with the challenges placed in her path."

Readers of the following memoir may judge for themselves.

—Cecil Dawkins, Santa Fe, fall 2001

1 ▌ MY EARLY DAYS

I'm sitting here enjoying the fireplace. I do that every day comes the wintertime. I think it's the most comfortable thing there is. Of course you always have to be jumping up putting wood in it. That's part of the game. But a fire is so much company.

How did I come to live in New Mexico? I came down through Trinidad in a Model T Ford Touring Car with my baby in a basket on the seat beside me. She was nine months old. I was running away from a rotten marriage. Climbing up the Raton Pass was no easy matter. The Model T refused to make it up that steep grade because the gas was gravity feed. So I rolled back to the bottom, put her in reverse, and backed all the way to the top. Once at the crest I turned around and coasted down into New Mexico, a place I'd never seen. It was the spring of 1921. I was twenty-two years old, older than New Mexico, which joined the Union in 1912 and would be home to me for the rest of my life.

I am going to try to tell you the story of my life, starting out with the history of my existence beginning back when I was hardly more than a baby, long before I ever thought of heading west.

I was born Frances Minerva Nunnery in Covington, Kentucky on

September 12, 1898, but the first thing I remember happened after we'd moved to Pittsburgh. The lady my mother had taking care of me dressed me up and told me we were going down to see a train go by because President McKinley had been killed.

When the long train came rolling through Pittsburgh, we were in the big crowd lining the railroad tracks. The train was all decorated in black drapes. I don't know where it came from, but it was on the Baltimore and Ohio Railroad. It seemed to me like whatever had happened was a terrible thing. Everybody was crying and carrying on like they thought the end of the world was coming. I was three years old, but I still remember it like it was yesterday, just a sorrowful impression I got as a child that's stayed with me the rest of my life.

I remember seeing a picture of me about that age, with pigtails, one hanging down on each side, kind of fuzzy looking, stringy looking, and I had on a pair of shoes I guess was handed down, looked like about three sizes too big and the toes all kicked out. I was sitting on a pair of steps. That's the only picture I ever saw of me when I was a little kid. I don't know what became of it.

I had two brothers, Carl and Lewis, and two sisters, all older and pretty well all grown up excepting Irene, the one about four years older than me. I really had a rough time with her. She gave me a lot of static. Once, when I was about three, they put a new dress on me and I went and slid down a muddy bank in it, didn't know any better. Well, my oldest sister, Arva, grabbed me by the arm and flung me down on the couch. Broke my arm. They had to take me to the hospital and get it set. After that it was in a sling.

We never had any affection whatsoever shown in our family, but Mother was partial to Irene. She said Irene was delicate. When Mother had her migraines, Irene was the one took care of her. I felt like an orphan.

After we moved to Pittsburgh, Nunnery, my father, got sick. He died when I was less than a year old. I later heard that George Nunnery's folks came from England as stowaways. I never heard anything else about my grandparents on either side. My mother married again when I was about three.

Mother was a striking-looking woman. Her maiden name was Amelia Jane Hill. My mother's second husband, Mr. Bichel, a widower, was a Pennsylvania Dutchman with a long handlebar mustache drooped over his upper lip. Once my mother married him he was my daddy, but my name was still Nunnery. It was confusing.

To my knowledge, my mother had two husbands, Nunnery and Bichel. I heard there was another one in there, Wilson, but I don't know when or if they were ever married. I heard he was killed logging up north somewhere.

The Dutchman Bichel had been out in Kansas wheat farming. As soon as they were married they took me and Irene on a train and we went to Kansas to my new stepfather's wheat farm. I remember a little about that trip, the sound of the wheels clacking, and passing through little towns at night, seeing lamplight in windows, kind of lonesome-looking, and Mother taking us out to walk up and down a platform while we waited on some siding—sidetracked, I guess that's where the term came from—for another train to go by.

Once we got to Kansas, whenever my stepfather was going out in the fields he took me with him. He let me sit on the mowing machine between his feet behind the team, and sometimes he let me ride on the work horses while they pulled the machinery around. I hung onto the hames hooked to the collar while the horse slogged across the field. And of course I enjoyed that, I thought that was great fun. And my stepdad let me ride one big old yellow horse by the name of Prince that had big furry ruffs around his pasterns like a Clydesdale.

They were always having these—cyclones, they called them. The wheat farm had a cyclone cellar. I never will forget it. Every time it come up one of these storms, they took me down in this hole in the ground. We stayed down in there till the cyclone was over, then came up to find out if we still had a house. They never got the house.

I was enjoying myself all right in Kansas, but Mother decided she wasn't going to stay any place where these storms kept on and on and the wind was so bad. Mother said, "I will not live in a place where the wind blows the hairpins out of my hair and the milk out of the pail after we milked it out of the cow. I am fed up with this place," or to that effect. My mother insisted her new husband get rid of the place and get it sold, which he did.

We only stayed in Kansas that one summer while my stepfather harvested a wheat crop that Will and Walter, his two sons by an earlier marriage, had tended for him while he was back east looking for a wife. I've heard that the actor Frederick March—his real name was Bichel—was Walter's son. Doris, my stepdad's daughter by that earlier marriage, became my lifelong friend.

So back we went to Pittsburgh. But we weren't there very long before Mother and Mr. Bichel decided they were going to move to Virginia and get into the tobacco business. So we moved down there to Dillon, Virginia and got a tobacco plantation of two hundred acres.

On the tobacco farm, we lived in a rented house while they put up a house made of yellow pine logs. The workmen first had to cut down the trees and strip the bark. It took a while for the house to be far enough along for us to live in the lower floor. The new house smelled pleasantly of fresh-cut wood. I can bring up that smell to this day if I put my mind to it.

On the farm we all had our own chores. Mine was hauling fresh cold water to the carpenters from the spring bubbling up out of white sand in the shade of a big old poplar. It made a little pond about the size of a double bed, and a ditch took the water off to the creek. The creek was wide and overhung by trees. It made a low muttering sound. If you didn't know better you'd think it was people off at a little distance carrying on a conversation. Over the spring we built a spring house with a boardwalk around it to put milk and butter in so they'd stay cool.

The carpenters never finished a bucket, so as the buckets were heavy—I had to carry them up the hill with both hands—I got to cheating on the trips to the spring. I'd go off a little way, then bring back the same bucket. Well, it was the middle of summer, and the water didn't stay cold for long. One of the men complained of the lukewarm water, and my mother got after me with a willow switch. It left my backside bloody. I took it. I knew I deserved it. I decided right then I would not lie again if there was a chance of being caught at it. That was my first whipping in Virginia, but it would not be the last. I got switched several times a week because Irene was forever telling lies and blaming things on me.

After the house was built, we put up cabins for the help. We had two families on our place. Aunt Mary Brooks and Aunt Nanny Woodson soon moved in with their husbands and children.

During haying or resetting the young tobacco plants, everybody worked in the fields, black and white alongside each other. On the plantation I was in the field with the Negroes all the time. People we call black people now we called Negroes then. Anyhow, I grew up with black people. We had these big tobacco fields and I worked out there with the help, a little bitty kid picking the worms and suckers off the tobacco plants.

Tobacco was the money crop, and growing tobacco was a year-round proposition. Work started in February, burning off the land to ready it for transplanting the tobacco shoots we'd already started in seed beds fertilized with good rotted manure and covered with cheesecloth and hemmed in by logs to keep out varmints.

After we got a heavy rain in May we transplanted them. The seedlings, three or four inches high by then, were easily uprooted and set out in the fields. We planted them three or four feet apart, and we had about forty acres in tobacco. The job took everybody working, my family and the Brooks and Woodsons, grownups and kids alike. Getting the plants in the field took about two weeks.

Once in the field, we had to chop the weeds and keep the dirt up around the little plants. When suckers started growing between the stalk and the leaf, they had to be pinched off. Otherwise, there'd be a lot of little tobacco leaves, none of the good big ones. I did a lot of suckering. By the time I was eight or nine years old, I was working in the fields from dawn to dusk.

We harvested when the plants were about three feet high with ten or twelve leaves and the bloom at the top was a cluster of small pink blossoms, which we cut off in the bud. The top leaves were about eight or ten inches long, and the middle leaves about a foot or longer. The bottom leaves, or lugs, made a cheap grade of tobacco. On each plant there were always six or eight good heavy leaves containing the most gum, or nicotine. They were used for cigars, or stogies, or good pipe tobacco.

Harvesting the tobacco plants meant splitting the stalk about halfway down with a tobacco knife, its blade sharp on both sides, then splitting it up from the bottom. Once the plant was cut off, two kids held long poles and the grownups hung the split stalks over the poles—not too close or they'd scald and the tobacco would be ruined. The poles were hauled into barns called stripping houses and hung in tiers from cross beams under the roof, one level above another. That's why tobacco barns tend to be tall.

From time to time a couple of men climbed up on the tier poles to regulate the stalks and keep the leaves from touching. We kept a fire of green wood burning on the dirt floor, under the tiers of tobacco, to smoke it till it was cured. Curing took about six weeks.

Then the stalks were taken down and stacked in a "bulk"—that's a pile about the size of a cord of wood, 4 by 4 by 8 feet. The leaves were covered with old rags and cloths, but the stack ends were left exposed. We sprinkled the exposed ends about twice a week to keep the leaves pliable.

Late November or early December all the workers, including the kids, started stripping the leaves from the bulks while one of the experts—always a black man—graded them. Then we tied them into "hands" and laid them into new bulks according to the grade—lugs, shorts, and longs (the best quality).

While we sat around after dark, sometimes till midnight, stripping the leaves off by lantern light and tying them in hands, the black people sang spirituals. I knew the words and sang right along with them. We'd all be nodding our heads and patting our feet in time with the singing. And they told ghost stories. Well of course I listened. Mother always told me children should be seen and not heard, so I grew up listening. I learned a lot that way. And we learn by mistakes. I've learned a lot by mistakes I've made.

Anyway, I set there in the lantern light, tying tobacco leaves into hands and listening to ghost stories, and I got too scared to go home. The house was only maybe two or three hundred yards away from the stripping house, but night after night somebody had to walk me home. They all teased me about it, but they never minded taking me, we were friends.

After Christmas, in January, the tobacco was loaded onto wagons and taken to the warehouse and sold to buyers. Then in February we'd burn off the fields and start the whole business over again.

The first Christmas I recall was on the tobacco farm. Mother said Christmas presents were a pagan custom, out of harmony with the solemn season. But this Christmas my stepdad gave me a little wooden cart he'd carved, with real wheels that turned. Mother said it would be the ruination of my character.

I heard at Sunday School about hanging up your stocking so Santa Claus could fill it Christmas Eve night with goodies, so I hung up a ragged one of mine. Christmas morning I stuck in my hand and came up with a smelly mess of ripe horse apples. My grownup brother Carl had put them there. He thought that was funny.

Carl was the oldest and he'd grown up without a father to keep him in line. Mother was the only one could do anything with him. He terrorized me with horror stories, especially stories about women tortured and murdered. He gave me nightmares. Being the bottom rung on the family ladder was pretty rough in those days.

At Christmas we had fried chicken and sweet potatoes and onions, and other vegetables flavored with sage and mustard and the ground-up roots of horseradish dug up from the big sand pile where Mother buried them to keep them from rotting. And we had apple pie made with apples from the root cellar.

Mother canned and dried all summer. So we might not have presents, but we always had a Christmas feast from the garden, especially if the preacher came to call, driving his one-horse buggy. The church was in Gravel Hill, the town closest to the farm, about fifty miles from Richmond. Gravel Hill was only the church, a few houses, a grocery story, and a post office.

The preacher always sat at the head of the table and got served the best of the eats, and us hungry kids just had to watch big-eyed and wait for the second setting and left-overs. But Mother was partial to preachers, as will be borne out later in my story. Me, I never had much use for them. It was Jesus who was my friend.

We always said the blessing before meals: Bless this food and us who eat it. And at night, before crawling between the quilts, I had to kneel by my bed with my hands together and say a prayer that scared me, so I always prayed it with my eyes clinched shut:

> Now I lay me down to sleep,
> I pray the Lord my soul to keep.
> If I should die before I wake,
> I pray the Lord my soul to take.

Meanwhile, Mother got herself pregnant. She had a little brother for me. Clifford. When Clifford got old enough to walk, he followed me everywhere. He bore a resemblance to his dad, even-tempered Mr. Bichel. I was no longer the lowest rung on the ladder, I finally had somebody to boss around. Clifford didn't mind. He became my accomplice in every mischief I thought up, and my ally against Irene.

In Virginia in the spring the dogwood trees smell sweet enough to make you drunk. It's a low tree, a hardwood. You can't kill it out, and the stumps never rot. Clifford and I liked to explore everywhere. We climbed around under the wild honeysuckle and Virginia creeper and found apples that had wintered under the vines still fresh and good to eat. There were whole fields of wild strawberries, and the old orchard was full of them. Just about every kind of berry grew on the place. The fences crawled with wild grapevines, and the swamp was full of wild water lilies. The men went possum hunting at night when foxfire glowed on swamp stumps and fallen logs.

Clifford and I got along pretty good together whenever this older sister wasn't beating on us. Irene always had the easiest tasks, and even at that she rarely did the dishes but left them in the sink attracting hoards of flies. But Mother never disapproved. She said Irene was peaked. She was supposed to have some mysterious ailment that sapped her energy. Sometimes I thought it would be nice to be sickly like Irene and have Mother nurse me.

Mother was a skilled practical nurse. Back in Pittsburgh she had often been off at her job at the Pest House—that's what they called the clinic that treated all kinds of diseases. And once we were down in Virginia she was soon traveling in every direction from Gravel Hill to visit the ailing, carrying medicinal herbs and mustard plasters she made herself from mustard seeds ground and mixed with flour. She spread the mix on a cloth and applied it to the skin. The concoction smelled like horseradish. Mother knew all about herbs.

I'd be working in the fields and see her pass in the buggy. I thought she looked grand, dressed in a hat and tailored suit. The skirts were long and dragged the ground, and hats were these big concoctions decorated with fruits and feathers and held on with long, dangerous hat pins to defy the wind. She'd be on her way to help some sick person, maybe to tap some poor old dropsied lady in order to start the urine. The doctors said she had healing hands. I was proud she was my mother.

But every time Mother left home, poor invalid Irene found some reason to beat us up and plenty of strength to do it. Whenever there was any housework to do or any dishes to wash, why, she went to the chick sales and sat there reading romance tripe till she was sure all the work was done.

One day we fixed her. Clifford and I found a bumblebee nest near the corner of the barn. Bumblebees nest in the ground, and we turned a fruit jar upside-down over the hole and caught all these bumble bees and put a lid on them that we'd punctured with nails so they'd get some air. Then we pried loose a plank at the back of the privy, in the bottom, and when Irene settled down in there we shoved it aside and turned the bees loose beneath her.

Irene came out in a hurry, screaming her head off and pulling her dress down over her drawers. And Mother came out on the porch yelling for us to show ourselves. Clifford—ever the good child—stepped out of hiding. That left nothing for me to do but step out after him and say I was to blame, he only did what I told him to.

Mother said, "You think I don't know that? I'm at my wit's end. I don't know what I'm going to do with you. Miss McCracken says you're the smartest one in the whole school so I know you know better." She'd sigh with her hand on her hip. "All right," she said. "Go fetch me a peach tree switch."

Clifford got a few licks, but I got a beating. I didn't cry. I counted it a matter of pride to stand there and take my medicine.

On the plantation we had two mule teams and a team of buggy horses. I longed to ride one of the jennies. Her name was Julie. She had a dark face with light circles around her eyes and nose like a mask. And she had long skinny white warts on her nose. One time Carl tried to pull them off, and she honked and reared back and bared her big teeth the color of yellow corn and sent him sprawling in the dirt. After that Julie had no use for white men. If one came anywhere near, she put her neck straight out and bared her teeth and went after him.

Couldn't anybody handle Julie but Benny. Benny was in charge of the mule team and the horses. His name was Benjamin James Portales Ramrodsman Poivatan Perval Woodson, but his little brother Henry had only that one name. Martha was their sister, Big Henry was their father, and Aunt Nanny was their mother.

My mother would look at me with her hands on her hips and say, "You're a sight! Run tell Aunt Nanny to get the rats' nests out of your hair."

And I'd run, and Aunt Nanny would laugh. "Law, chile, yo' hair ain't like no white girl's." She untangled my hair and braided it again, and that lasted for several days.

I finally sweet-talked Benny into letting me get on Julie's back. He said she liked me, he could tell. So he put me up and walked alongside in case Julie decided to bolt. I learned to ride her. In time I rode everything on the place, including the buggy horses. I'd grab hold of anything I could reach. I climbed tails and clambered up legs. It's a wonder I didn't get kicked to hell and gone. But most animals are tolerant of the young.

We went to church in the two-seater buggy or the four-seater surrey. But sometimes I rode Julie to Sunday School and tied her to a tree till it let out.

Benny was a great tall guy. He didn't have to climb on the wheel hub to get in the wagon, he just lifted his leg and stepped in. Benny always left a black whip in the wagon to crack over the team of mules to get them started.

Well, there were lots of snakes in Virginia. There were copperheads, copper colored and two feet long, in the barns and machine sheds, and cottonmouths a yard long in the river. When we went swimming they stuck their heads out of the water and opened their mouths at us like telling us to get out of their territory and leave them alone, only they had no voice or else it was too small for us to hear. The inside of their mouths really was white as cotton.

Anyway, one day Clifford and I took Benny's whip out of the wagon and put in a black snake we'd killed. When Benny stepped in the wagon and reached for his whip, he picked up this big black snake instead. He let out a yell must have been heard two valleys over and jumped out of the wagon, and the team took off and tore the wagon all to hell and tore up the harness, too. Of course we both got a good paddling out of that.

Benny had to cross a boardwalk over the creek every morning coming to work. The creek was maybe about twenty-five feet across. So after we saw he was scared of snakes, one evening Clifford and I killed a water snake and laid it across the foot bridge.

When Benny saw it he wouldn't cross the bridge. He threw rocks at the snake and tried to shoo it off, but of course that snake wouldn't budge. So Clifford and I rescued Benny. We went out on the bridge and chopped up the snake with a hoe and killed it all over again.

We liked playing tricks on Benny because he was gullible, but once he realized what we were up to he laughed right along with us. He never held anything against us. We pulled a few raw things, Clifford and I. We were always up to something.

You had to be pretty self-sufficient on a plantation then. We made our own soap by boiling lard and lye. At first it came out soft, but then it hardened and we cut it into cakes. And our wooden bedsteads were homemade with holes drilled in the two-by-six sides and rope strung through them for springs. We made our nightdresses from flour sacks, and we slept on straw tick mattresses we stuffed ourselves.

Bedbugs bred in the poplar trees, and in the summer we were plagued by them. They have a peculiar sour smell and leave red spots where they bite you. They crawled along seams of the mattresses, so we painted the seams and the bedsteads with kerosene to kill them off. I sometimes snuck out on the roof and slept there to get away from them. They weren't bad in the winter.

Hay cutting started in midsummer, June or July. We grew timothy for the horses and sweet clover for the cows because timothy and sweet clover reseed themselves. We generally got two cuttings, maybe two and a half if the frost held off. The mower was a long blade hitched to the cog of the wheel that drove it back and forth, cutting the hay.

Once it was cut, the hay rake, a long piece of machinery with wheels at each end and metal fingers suspended in between, raked the hay into windrows. When a row was full, a foot on a pedal raised the rake to start another row. The men drove wagons into the field and forked the hay from the rows onto the wagon beds and took it to the barn, then stood in the wagon and forked it up to the man in the loft window, who kept moving it farther back in the loft, making room for more.

When I was old enough I rode the mowing machine, sitting on the seat behind the team. One day I was riding the mower with Crawley Brooks, Aunt Mary's son, when he got off to raise the blade over a stump. Instead of using the safety device on the end of the blade that picked it up, he picked up the blade by hand.

Well, the blade fell back and came down on his finger, left it hanging only by a thread of flesh. Crawley screamed. Blood was pouring out of him on the hay. I jumped down and raced toward the houses, yelling for Aunt Mary. She was forking hay over where the rake piled it into rows for the wagons. When she heard me, she looked up and dropped the fork and came running, and I led her to Crawley. He was writhing on the ground, holding onto his mutilated hand.

When Aunt Mary saw his finger she scratched a hunk of resin off the nearest pine, joined her son's stump and the severed finger back together, then wrapped the gum around them, telling me to run break her off some good straight twigs. I asked no questions, I did as I was told. She used the twigs as splints, lining them up alongside the finger, then tore off a strip of her petticoat and bandaged Crawley's hand.

Well, it grew back. The graft left only a white scar circling Crawley's dark finger. Like my mother, Aunt Mary Brooks was a woman who in any emergency knew what to do and how to do it.

My mother had a saying:

> If a task is once begun,
> Never leave it till it's done.
> Be the labor great or small,
> Do it well or not at all.

In the fall of the year, while the women were busy drying or canning food from the garden to feed their families all winter, I walked barefoot three miles to school every day in my flour-sack dress, carrying my shoes. You had to save your shoes. You only put them on once you got to school.

School was a one-room log house. There were eight or ten of us in there, all levels together. In those days all school mistresses were women. Our school mistress was squinchy dried-up Miss Annie McCracken. Miss McCracken was always nice to me.

I did well in school. We read about Chicken Little thinking the sky was falling and running to tell Henny Penny, when it was just a rose petal fell on her tail. I mastered McGuffey's Reader, and I memorized every verse of "The Ride of Jennie McNeill." I can say every word of it to this day, ninety years later. Jenny McNeill was a little girl, but she was a true heroine, just like Paul Revere, riding through the night to tell the people the British were coming. Why should men get all the glory?

But school didn't last all year. It was dismissed when the children were needed on the farm to help with planting or harvest.

Aside from tobacco, we raised a crop of sugar cane. In the fields it looks like maize. In the fall of the year, when the tops were brown and full of seeds and the leaves started turning yellow, a whole bunch of us would go in and strip the cane. Then we'd cut off the cane at the bottom with homemade cane knives made out of split sticks two or three feet long with a blade of sharpened metal stuck in the slot and fastened with wang. The cones and seeds went to the hogs, and the leaves to the cattle. On a farm you use everything, you never let anything go to waste.

The cane stalk sours if you don't tend to it right away. We processed the stalks by running them through the hammer mill, which chopped them up. Then we put them in a keg with a press like a wringer that pressed out the juice into a trough that took it to a cooking vat with a wood fire underneath that brought the juice to a boil.

We boiled it till it was a thick, dark syrup, then skimmed it off about a half-inch deep into pans and let it harden. Once it was hard we beat it up with wooden mallets and ground some for sugar and kept the rest to make molasses for pouring on pancakes.

In time my stepdad got malaria and Mother had to take him back to Pennsylvania on account of his health. Clifford and I stayed on the tobacco plantation another couple years with my oldest sister Arva and Grover, the man she'd married. Grover's family lived on a nearby farm. They made ice cream every Sunday and sometimes invited the neighbors. They cut the ice from the creek in winter and kept it in a cellar covered with sawdust so they'd have it in the summertime.

Anyway, in time Arva married Grover. I liked the ice cream a lot better than I liked Grover.

All over Virginia they used rock walls for line fences. They picked the rocks out of the fields to clear them, and stacked them up and walled their fields with them. One day when Clifford and I were digging into one of those old Colonial walls, we found a possum and dug it out. It was real fat. We took it home with us and fixed a wire cage out of a chicken coop that would do till we could build it a house. Turned out she had a bunch of babies in her pocket. When they popped out they didn't have any hair on them. Just little naked things.

We were real proud of our possum. We thought we really had something. We were feeding her and taking care of her and her children till along came my brother-in-law. He was a possum and coon hunter, and he decided we weren't going to keep our possum. So he snuck out there one night and turned her out. That made us pretty mad.

Grover had a special hunting dog he called Old Nan. He always let her in the house whenever it was cold, and she'd lay down by the stove, so he wouldn't let us kids stick our feet up there to warm them. We were unhappy about that situation. So one day when we went to get some corn or wheat ground for flour—that was the way you got your flour, you took your grain to the mill and had it ground—we took Old Nan over to the mill with us in the wagon and threw her in the mill race.

It was November. The water was colder'n hell. Once we realized what we'd done, we ran downstream and fished her out and dried her off with our clothes. We took good care of her after that. But to this day I feel sorry about that poor old dog. We took out on Old Nan what we ought to've taken out on Grover. We should have thrown Grover in the millrace.

Julie the mule didn't care for Grover any more than we did because he was always teasing her. If she was in her stall, whenever he walked by the barn she knew it was him, and she raised hell kicking the side of the barn.

One day when I was riding her, she went after Grover and treed him like his hound treed possums. Then she went to grazing. Julie and I just stayed there in the shade under the branches and kept Grover treed for some time, till his squalling brought Arva out of the house. She broke off a branch and came after me. Julie and I had to run so Grover could climb down—it was that or have Arva beating up on me.

One day I was riding Julie past the church during prayer meeting, all those people in there whining to the Lord. Well, the church doors were wide open—it was summertime—and I rode Julie up the steps and through the doors and down the aisle on one side, across the front, then up the aisle on the other. For once the preacherman was silenced. Prayer meeting came to a halt, all eyes on Julie and me.

Don't ask me why I did it. I don't know. I went to bed without my supper that night.

Things sort of drifted along and first thing I know another spring set in, and then it was summertime again. Arva was pregnant, about to have another baby—she already had two—and I'm laying out in the hammock on the front porch—I was about twelve years old—

when along comes Grover and straddles the hammock and crawls on top of me.

I knew what that meant. I'd never seen the genitals of a man, but I knew it was what the horses and cows and pigs did, and I didn't need that. I reared up and kicked him where it did the most good and rolled out of the hammock and got rid of him. Then I went and told Arva.

Well, she said it was my fault, I had no business laying out there in that hammock. And she got ahold of my mother up in Pennsylvania and raised hell about it, told her I was growing into a hellion.

That's how come Clifford and I got sent back to my mother and my stepdad and left Arva and Grover there on the farm, which they finally got. My mother turned it over to them. Clifford and I never got anything out of it.

So we got on a train and started back to Pennsylvania—another long trip on a train, though the trips to and from Kansas were longer. I was half asleep when we got into Washington, D.C. All of a sudden the train bumped—they must have been hooking some cars together—and I sat straight up and hollered, "Whoa, mule!" Everybody on the train turned around and looked at me and laughed. I thought I was driving mules. Whenever you said 'Whoa' to our team of mules, they pulled up and jerked the wagon so they could rest in their collars. Everybody on the train got a kick out of that. Down in Virginia I drove mules and oxen and everything else I could climb aboard.

So we get to Pittsburgh. Mother and my stepdad were renting a place over a bakery called The Duesenberry Pie Company, just off Forbes Street. It smelled good all the time. Irene found a boyfriend, Robert Ott, down there in the bakery. He was a delivery boy. We ate quite a few good pies. That's all he ever gave her, not candy or jewelry or flowers. This romance went on till she married him. Irene was finally out of our hair. Clifford and I were glad to be shut of her.

2 | MY FIRST PAYING JOB

In those days you went to work as a kid. We didn't have any child labor laws or that kind of thing, so when I got to be about thirteen—that would be about 1911—I went to work in the Iron City Laundry, shaking out barber towels before they went in the washing machines. That was the only job I could get as I had no prior experience.

The laundry was hot and steamy. It was one long room always humming and droning with the machines, eight or ten mangles and ironing boards. The women working them were on their feet all day. There was no such thing as rest breaks.

When I complained to the forelady about hairs from the barber towels getting in my mouth, she told me to keep my mouth shut. When I objected that they still got in my eyes and nose and all over my face, she said, "See that window over there?"

I said I did.

"Well," she said, "go up there and they'll give you a pink slip."

I thought I was getting paid, but turned out I was getting fired. That was my first experience of a job and it lasted about a day and a half.

My second was at H. J. Heinz. The Heinz plant covered a couple of city blocks. The buildings were connected by covered bridges over the street. H. J. Heinz had this pickle department, and peanut butter department, and ketchup department, and beanery—a department for each thing they put up. To get from one building to the next you went through these raised alleyways over the street. You never had to go out in the street. First they put me on a table with a bunch of other gals putting pickles in bottles. You sat up there on a high stool with a long stick, and you poked in the pickles. They all had to be in certain places in the bottles and the bottles were inspected to see if you got all the pickles right. I didn't do too good at that job because I got pickles in every which-way. So the lady in charge decided maybe I would do all right putting labels on the bottles.

The bottles came by on a belt, and workers stuck the labels on by hand. But I had trouble with that, too. When I put these strips around the neck they never met on the other side, so they never passed inspection. So she took me off that and finally asked me what I thought I could do. Well, I saw these capping machines that you set the bottle in and put your foot down on a peddle and it comes chomping down and hits the top of the lid and puts it on the bottle. I thought I could do that, so she let me try.

By the time I had squashed a half-dozen bottles, and had pickles scattered all over the floor and broken glass everywhere, she decided she couldn't put up with that, I was too destructive. So she made me an errand girl.

She took me over to the office. I looked at all these fancy dressed-up people and all these ladies beating on typewriters, and she explained to me that I was supposed to take orders from the office to each individual section, like the peanut butter department, or the beanery, or the pickle department or spaghetti department. I'd get a handful of these slips and then I'd wander around.

One day I was standing in this big wide corridor not knowing how to get to where I was supposed to go, just standing there looking like a lost cat and hoping nobody would notice when this gent comes up to me and says, "What's the matter, little girl, are you lost?"

I said no, I was looking for the peanut butter department.

"Well," he said, "you're standing in the middle of it."

There I was, right in the middle of the peanut butter department and didn't have the sense to know it. That sometimes happens in life. You're right in the middle of where you're going and not the sense to know it. Well, he directed me around till I got straightened out, and later I come to find out this gent was a bigwig of the H. J. Heinz Company. I got to doing pretty well with that job, carrying these orders around.

Then there come a time when H. J. Heinz created their own entertainment, a natatorium for the help. One day the office force was to go swimming in the natatorium. So I go over there with all the rest like I'm supposed to. They gave us these bathing suits that come from your knees all the way up to your neck, and they told me to put on one of these things. So I did. And to come out and get in the pool. So I done this. I got the bathing suit on, and I hid in there a long time, too embarrassed to come out. When finally one of the help pushed me out of there, I was so ashamed I ran right over and jumped into nine foot of water. That's when I realized I didn't know how to swim.

Well, I panicked and sank to the bottom, and I saw this thing that they pull up to let the water out, and I saw it was my only hope. I was fighting my way over to this gadget to empty that pool so I wouldn't drown when a man dove in and grabbed me by the bathing suit and yanked me out of there.

"You little fool," he said, "if you couldn't swim why'd you jump into nine-foot of water?"

But it was too late to talk about it, I'd already done it. If I'd managed to pull out the plug, I'd have been down the Allegheny River.

Meanwhile my stepdad, who was a veterinarian by profession—he'd just been experimenting with wheat farming out in Kansas—went to work for the Harmon Dairy Company, a big outfit that delivered milk and cream and other dairy products all over Pittsburgh. They didn't have trucks in those days, and my stepdad took care of the dairy cows and the horses that pulled the Harmon Dairy Company's wagons around town.

And Mother had gone into the interior decorating business. She rented a store building out on Lincoln Avenue. So we moved from our place over the bakery out to East Pittsburgh. The buildings out there were so close together, just six or eight inches apart, you couldn't even walk between them.

This store building Mother had rented had three or four rooms upstairs, which is where we slept, and a big kitchen in back, which is where we cooked and ate. In the big store room downstairs she had samples of draperies and wall papers and anything else for decorating a house. Mother was a very capable woman. She'd tackle anything. People would come in and order what they wanted, and she would go ahead and get the job done.

Of course I was still at H. J. Heinz. I was there for a year or two. But I didn't like that job. I wanted to go to Westinghouse and apply for a job there, but I had a problem. I had to give Mother all the money I made, and she would give me one streetcar check to go to work and one streetcar check to come home. If I got off the streetcar in-between, why, I didn't have a check to get me back on. But finally I took the bull by the headlights and stopped off at the Westinghouse plant. I got a job there right away.

But the plant was about three or four miles from where we lived. I'd used up my return-trip check, so I had to walk all the way home. I got home late and Mother wanted to know why, so I just told her I'd missed the streetcar I usually came home on. For some time she didn't know I was working at Westinghouse.

I did well at Westinghouse because I was pretty mechanically inclined. I was learning how to make coils and motors and generators, and I was winding armatures. I found that very interesting. I gave all the money I made to my mother to save up for me to go to college and law school, though she didn't agree with that plan. She said law school was no place for a woman, a woman was supposed to go into either nursing or school teaching. I kept my mouth shut, but I wasn't having any of that.

Meanwhile my stepdad wasn't getting any better. He finally had to quit his job at the dairy company. He bought a farm up in Butler County, about forty miles outside of Pittsburgh, and moved up there. In the summertime when Clifford was not in school, he'd go up there and stay with his dad.

My stepdad had bought a team of horses that the milk company was retiring, and he'd taken them up to the farm. But one of the horses turned out to be balky and no good for farm work, so now he wanted me to come up there and bring it back to Pittsburgh to the dairy. I went up there on the bus, and I got up at about three the next morning and rode this horse all morning and all afternoon, all the way back to Pittsburgh in one day. I got it back to the dairy company at about dark.

The horse died that night. I guess I rode him too far. I felt terrible about that horse, but it was too late for that. It was done and I couldn't do anything about it.

When my stepdad got worse, Mother moved up to the farm to take care of him. She rented a room with light housekeeping facilities from a lady up the street, and she left Clifford there with me to go to school in the wintertime.

That lasted for a couple of years. I paid the rent out of my wages at Westinghouse, and I had to give Mother the rest to make the payments on the farm. I didn't mind. I was a good employee. I was already an instructor in coil armature winding. I was making pretty good money. My mother said, "After this war's over, then you can take the money and go to school."

I meant to go to law school, though I hadn't even gone through grade school. The only schooling I got was in that log cabin one-room school house with maybe eight or ten others, all ages. I learned to read and write, and I learned American history from Miss Annie McCracken.

I was at Westinghouse all through World War I, and I stayed there till 1919 when my health broke down. It was the time of the big flu epidemic that killed soldiers and civilians alike. Like a lot of people, I contracted tuberculosis. Westinghouse wanted to send me out to Denver, where they had a branch. They had their own doctors and medical plans out there, and they would pay my fare.

This brings the story of my life up to the time I left the East.

3 | I HEAD WEST

But Mother had a little different plan for me.

Mother said, "If you're going to have to go out west, you can't go out there by yourself." That's how she decided to get me married off to this preacher person from Colorado who had been going to school there in Pittsburgh at the Bible Institute. That's where my mother knew him. But I didn't know him. I'd only seen him once. We took a walk in Shenley Park, looked at the dinosaurs in the Museum. I guess Mother thought I would probably be safe out west married to a preacher. So I went out there on the train and he met me in Denver.

When you go to a place as celebrated as Denver, you expect to see a city. Didn't look like much of a city to me. There were street cars, not many passenger cars, lots of horses and wagons and buggies and people crowding the streets. But there weren't hardly any big buildings at all. Even covered night and day in smoke from the coke ovens on the hills, Pittsburgh was a big town with tall buildings and cobbled streets. After Pittsburgh, Denver looked very primitive, like somebody had mashed the whole town into the ground. I learned this preacher and I were going to live with his people up at Timnath, Colorado. That ended any hope of treatment by the Westinghouse doctors in Denver, which was my whole reason for heading west in the first place, but there I was. And as Timnath was some way off, we had to get married right away in Denver because single girls in those days didn't go running around spending the night on the road with some guy she wasn't married to.

This preacher claimed his marital rights that first night. And that was the worst experience of my life, this marriage business. I couldn't take it. I was so damn stupid I didn't know about those things. I'd lived on the farm and I thought people did like the animals—when you got ready to have a calf you took the cow to the bull, so when you wanted to have a child you had the sex act. Well of course that very first night I found out that wasn't so. It was a different situation altogether. And that was the beginning of the worst time of my whole life.

So here I was, living in Timnath in back of his parents' house in a little frame shack with a privy, when what I'd come west for was treatment in Denver for my tuberculosis. This preacher's name was Elmer Parker, and he was very vain. He had good teeth and a beautiful head of red-blond hair that he put up in waves at night. He beat egg whites and put his comb in it and ran it through his hair. Then he patted his waves in place and tied a rag over his head to keep them set for church the next day. I had no use for such as that. And I never could do anything to suit his mother. I wasn't her idea of a model wife. Right from the first I knew I had to get out of there.

With seven hundred and fifty dollars I had saved in Liberty Bonds while I was working for Westinghouse, pretty soon I bought a Model T Ford Touring Car. The car was mine but I didn't know how to drive it. Parker was supposed to be a Sunday School missionary, a sort of circuit preacher. He right away took over my car to do his circuit riding. I made up my mind I'd go along and watch what he did and learn how to drive a car.

He drove all around up in Colorado to these outlying farms, where people gave him food. And he took it from them instead of working and buying his own food himself. Every time Parker got some of these groceries from these poor farmers or some widow woman, he said the Lord was supplying his needs. I told him he ought to go out and work and supply his own needs. I told him the Bible says man will earn his bread by the sweat of his brow.

When this little old lady living way out to hell and gone in a dugout with a sod roof, flowers growing out the top, took down the one little old skinny ham shank she had hanging in her dugout house in a feed sack and gave it to him, he took it.

I was waiting in the Model T. When he brought it out and flung it in my lap, I dumped it on the floor. I told him I wasn't going anywhere in that car with that thing. I told him to take it back.

He said it was her offering, her widow's mite, he couldn't insult her by not accepting it, it was all she had.

I said I knew it was all she had. I said she didn't have to give him the last bite of meat she had in the house. Then I fished the ham shank off the floor of the car and got out with it.

He grabbed me by the arm and said, "You will not return that. You will not humiliate me in the presence of my congregation."

"Congregation!" I said. "A poor old lady and the jackrabbits."

"She's watching us!" Parker hissed. And he reminded me that a woman's place was at her husband's feet.

I told him to save it for his sermons, and I pushed past him and took the ham back to the old woman in her little sod dugout.

The old lady didn't want to take back the ham. She said she wanted to give it to the Lord. I told her the Lord knew it was the thought that counts. So she gave me two fruit jars of tumbleweed salad. Said she'd picked the sprouts when they were close to the ground and juicy, and she had plenty more.

Hers wasn't much of a life, but I thought at that time it was better than mine. Here I'd been an independent working woman, but now I belonged to this damn hypocrite. A hundred dollars a month was all he got. No wonder we were living in the shack in back of his folks' house. I was making three times that much from my job at Westinghouse before the TB got me.

Parker wasn't speaking to me when he turned the crank and climbed in the car, and I was glad to be shut of the conversation. I went back to watching how he put in the clutch and moved the throttle. The throttle was on the steering wheel. And I learned by watching that reverse was in the middle and the brake was on the right. Pretty soon when he wasn't at home I was practicing, driving around and around the backyard by the sheep pens.

And I learned how to take care of the car. I watched Parker put grinding compound around the valve hole of the engine block and rotate the valves back and forth to smooth the edges and get rid of old carbon deposits. The preacher hated getting his hands dirty, so pretty soon that was my job. I came to understand all about the cam shaft and the crank shaft that raised and lowered the pistons. Back in those days you had to be your own mechanic.

I was born liking to fish. All those mountains around, with their mountain streams, Parker only took me fishing up there once. But his folks' place backed up to the Poudre River. It was polluted with the pulp of the sugar beet refinery. The pollution made the fish taste nasty, so nobody fished and the fish proliferated.

I was so lonesome living in Timnath, Colorado that one day I put a string and a hook on a cane pole and caught an old carp. It had a little pursy sucker mouth and flat, staring eyes. I put it in a natural spring that come up out of the ground back there in a screen of low bushes. When nobody was watching, I would go back there and visit with my carp and take it something to eat, like crumbs or oatmeal flakes. And I would talk to it, "Hello, fish."

Parker's mother had birthed eleven, the last one during her change and it never developed. They called him 'the idiot.' The poor thing got in the habit of following me everywhere.

I knew he was there before I saw him. He was standing in the bushes watching me with the fish.

I asked him, "How'd you get out? Come on," I said, "back to the house before you fall in the river and drown."

Well, somehow one day the poor thing led Parker to the water hole in the bushes. The preacher yelled at me for polluting the spring and threw my fish back in the river.

That was okay. I was going to put the old fish back in the river anyway. That fish was the only pet I had in Colorado.

I'd told Parker I didn't want any children, partly because of my health, which was why I was out west in the first place though I never got any treatment, and partly because when I married this preacher I'd had in mind a missionary career, traveling to distant lands and helping the people. It was with that thought in my head that, after my days on the job at Westinghouse, I'd attended the Bible Institute nights.

But the missionary career was not to be, and of course he never let me alone. He told me it was a sin for a woman to deny her husband and there were ways to avoid pregnancy. I somehow got him to limit himself to once a week, and he withdrew in time to plant his slime on my belly. As soon as he was snoring, I got up and went out to the pump and washed myself in the cold water.

But in spite of that and in spite of the TB, after about two months I got pregnant. As soon as it was showing, he wouldn't take me anymore on his trips to save souls. He'd been mighty insistent on his husband's rights, but he was ashamed to show the proof of his lust. That disgusted me.

I lost all my energy. I stayed sick to my stomach for months, and I was frequently torn apart with coughing spasms from the TB. Parker's mother told me she'd produced ten healthy and one idiot without such foolishness.

When my time came I was in labor for twenty-four hours before they finally called a doctor. Parker's mother was against that, too. She said I was just stubborn and wouldn't cooperate. She said she'd had hers without help and so had everybody else she knew. She said I didn't want the child and that's why it couldn't get born.

When the old doctor finally came he took one look and saw how things stood. He put me on the buggy seat and covered me with a horse blanket and took me to the hospital. I lost consciousness on the way.

It turned out my hips were too narrow. Finally they had to take the baby with instruments. By then I'd been in labor thirty-six hours. It's a wonder I didn't die. But the upshot was, I had this little girl. I named her Anita.

And right after I had her, before the week was out, before I even got out of bed from getting over the hard birth, Parker was after me. He took to chasing me through the house naked as the day he was born. I finally grabbed a butcher knife and told him if he touched me I'd kill him.

The mother-in-law declared I'd lost my mind. She said they'd better do something about my demonic possession and get the devil cast out of me. They got a preacher from another church to come around. He was supposed to perform some kind of exorcism, but I mustered strength enough to chase him out of the shack with a frying pan. Then I put a slide bolt I'd bought earlier in Fort Collins on the bedroom door and locked myself away from everybody.

Parker would lay out there praying out loud, asking God to soften my heart. I told him it wasn't my heart, it was something on him that needed softening. I told him to go take a cold bath, turn some cold water on himself. I told him, "You dirty son of a bitch, you're supposed to be a man of God, but you're nothing but a no-good rapist." I told him, "Whenever I get over this birth and get my strength back I'm leaving you. I'm not staying in this situation." And I meant it.

Parker was finally leaving me alone. He'd found a blond diversion. I knew he was chasing one of the girls in the choir, and about this time he got one of the mission teachers pregnant. She came to me pitiful and told me he'd got her in a family way. Asked me what she should do about it.

I told her the preacher had refused me a divorce on religious grounds, so I guess he couldn't marry her and make an honest woman of her.

The poor thing had to leave town. I never knew if she had the baby or what happened to it if she did. Parker of course hadn't done anything wrong. He said the woman was already fallen or she wouldn't have given in to him.

Well, I hid the car keys and turned a deaf ear to his begging for the Model T. I made him leave my car at home. When he went off preaching his circuit in his parents' horse and buggy, I fixed up the touring car to where I could sleep in it and camp in it. I sawed off the tops of the seats so I could put a bed across them at night for me and my kid, and I attached to the outside of the car a little cabinet I'd made with shelves for food stuffs and staples. I hinged the door at the bottom, so when you opened it you had a little work bench or a table. I carried the baby's groceries on my own person, all she would need for a while, and I planned to provision myself along the road.

In those bad days I consoled myself thinking of all the money my mother was holding for me. It would be the thing to get me out of my present situation. But when it came time for her to send me my money, it turned out my mother had used all of it to pay off the mortgage on the farm. So nothing left to do but cash in the last of my Liberty Bonds, which I did as soon as I could get out and around. I stashed the money in the bottom of a gallon jar of pinto beans. The baby was coming along fine. I had plenty of milk and she was putting on weight and starting to jabber. So I bided my time, waiting out the Colorado winter.

At last spring finally came. Anita was about nine months old. I dug what cash I had left out of the gallon jar, provided myself with a little from the larder, put the baby in a basket on the seat beside me, and I picked up and left this preacher. I couldn't stand him. I aimed to start a new life.

The highways at that time were just washboardy dirt roads. You had to carry extra gasoline with you, buying it in whatever town you could get it. I left Colorado with two five-gallon cans of gas, and I filled up in Denver and again in Pueblo, Colorado, at that time a steel and mining town. There weren't any filling stations, just country stores that had pumps with that glass business up at the top. You could see the gasoline in it and see it gurgling while you filled your tank. The Model T's gas tank was under the driver's seat. You had to remove the cushion and put your measuring stick into the tank, then put in the gasoline hose.

Cars were simple in those days. I knew all there was to know about that Model T Ford. If something went wrong, why I knew how to fix it. There wasn't much to go wrong. You had to clean the plugs every now and then, and the points and magneto—the lights were magneto-operated. That's about all.

We came down through Trinidad. But as the gas was gravity feed, when the road started climbing it wouldn't run into the engine. Up a little way and the car kept stalling out. I had to figure out something or be stuck on the wrong side of the mountain. So I rolled back down, turned the car around, and put it in reverse. And, sure enough, it chugged backward right up that mountain. I backed all the way up that steep grade. Then at the top I turned around and entered Raton Pass head-on and coasted down into a place where they spoke another language. Some thought it was a foreign country. The year was 1921. I was twenty-two years old, older than New Mexico, which only became a state in 1912.

4 | A RUNAWAY WIFE

It took me two days to get from Las Vegas to Taos. It was dark when I got down to the foot of US Hill. I didn't know how far it was to Taos, so I decided to camp where I was. I pulled off beside the Little Rio Grande in the canyon above Ranchos de Taos.

I must have come into Taos down the same road Blumenschein and Phillips, those earliest of the Taos painters, took back in 1898, the year I was born. It was a few days before I was born that their wagon broke down just north of Taos. I heard they flipped a coin to see who would unhitch the horse and ride into town for help getting their wagon fixed. Phillips won the toss (or lost it, depending on the horse), and he liked the place so much he talked Blumenschein into settling in Taos instead of going on to Old Mexico.

While I was setting up camp here comes an old Mexican couple with a team and wagon. They pulled in there and made camp, too, in the clearing by the river. The old lady came over and picked up the baby and took her out of the car, all the time trying to talk to me in Spanish. That scared me. I didn't know what they were going to do. Maybe they were going to kidnap the baby.

But she rocked Anita in her arms and got her to grip a finger with her little hand, and I finally caught on she just liked the baby. She fixed something to eat in a big iron skillet and insisted that I eat with them. Tired as I was, I was happy to oblige.

The next morning the Spanish lady got up and fixed pork and eggs and tortillas for breakfast, and they fed me again. Then her husband turned their horses loose and, when I'd made up the bed in the car, they just came on over and climbed in the back seat. The old man slapped with his hands like shoving flies off his knees and said, "*Vamos a Taos.*" I figured that meant, "Let's go to Taos."

So we went to Taos.

Taos was just a little old mud town then, hardly any buildings were stuccoed. The street around the plaza was just dirt, and crowded with horses and wagons and saddled horses tied up to the hitching posts. Pretty soon a bunch of Spanish people crowded around the Model T. I'd never been around Spanish people before, never heard the language. At first I was afraid of them, but finally I realized that all they wanted was for me to ride them around the plaza in the car, and for half a day that's what I did. First one group and then another, I rode people around and around Taos plaza in the Ford. I guess it was one of the first cars ever seen in the streets of Taos.

Low on money, later I went into the Columbian Hotel to see if I could get a restaurant job. But when I saw a rough-looking bunch of cowboys in the lobby playing poker, I decided this wasn't the kind of place my mother would want me to be. The owner, a man named Pooler, had some time before been shot by a drifter claimed to be a traveling watch repairman who'd been kicked out of the bar earlier for being drunk and disorderly.

The Columbian hotel was just a one-story affair faced up to the south side of the plaza. It was the principal hotel in Taos until Don Fernando opened up in 1926. Later the Karavas brothers remodeled it, but they ran it as the Columbian Hotel for some years before rechristening it La Fonda de Taos. However, I didn't know all this at that time.

I spent the day with the old couple. They loaded up with groceries, and I bought a few little staples and fingered warm blankets I couldn't afford. Then late afternoon I brought them back up the canyon. We all slept there by the river that night.

The next morning they caught their horses and hitched up the team and took off back to Mora or over the hill to Peñasco, or wherever they were going, and since Taos was a rough place then, full of bars and saloons, I headed south. It was an all-day trip down the narrow, muddy, steep and twisting canyon road alongside the Rio Grande, then through the Española Valley with the Jemez Mountains off to the west and on into Santa Fe.

My mother had been in Santa Fe in the early days, before any of us were born, just my oldest brother, because Nunnery, my father, had been an engineer on the Santa Fe Railroad when it was put through New Mexico. While the railroad was being laid out, she and Nunnery were out here following the railroad gang. Mother had smelled the sage and lived in adobe houses and seen the buttes and mesas and New Mexico sunsets. From my father and mother I must have inherited New Mexico in my blood. It felt like coming home.

When I arrived in Santa Fe, there wasn't any pavement, not even around the plaza, but it was the oldest state capital in the country. When it had the choice between being the home of the state university or the state penitentiary, it chose the penitentiary. I'm not sure what that tells you about Santa Fe. Anyhow, I looked the little adobe town over, then drove on through, heading for Albuquerque. And found there was only eight blocks of pavement in Albuquerque. A whole big city with only eight blocks of pavement.

Well, it was summer by then, and the weather was warm. I kept on running around the state trying to find a place to settle down. The baby was a pretty good baby, not crying much or anything. She didn't give me any trouble. Lucky for me she was still nursing. That didn't cost anything and I didn't have much money left. I washed diapers in every stream I came to and hung them on piñon trees or sage bushes or laid them on rocks to dry. She was starting to crawl and trying to pick herself up and walk by then. If we hadn't been living in the car, I'd've let her go naked and just washed her behind instead of the diapers, like the Indian mothers did.

I was picking up small jobs where I could. I worked for a while on an old Pueblo Indian ruin they later called Pecos Monument. These guys were digging around in there looking for what they could find in the way of old Indian things, pots and all. I worked there for fifty cents a day. You had to dig very careful, just picking at things. If you found something, you called this guy over and he went at it with a little fine brush till he got it out. While I worked, an old Indian lady looked after Anita, but ever so often I ran out and nursed her.

I was still exploring on my own, running around the state in the Model T looking for a place to settle. One day when I was camping out in the piñon trees on top of a bluff and the baby was asleep in the car, I climbed down one of these old pole Indian ladders and crawled around in some caves dug in the cliffs. Their ceilings were still black from the smoke of cooking fires, and pictures had been scratched in some of them of stick men and snakes and peculiar forms I couldn't name.

In the back of one of the caves I came upon something scared me. It was all dried up, just skin and bones, a dead baby strapped up in some old feathers. It had long hair, and teeth. About 20–25 inches long. Maybe a two-year-old child.

I took it out of there and brought it straight back to Santa Fe and gave it to the museum. The body was all there. It was mummified. That happened in Frijoles Canyon, now called Bandelier National Monument.

Finally in my wanderings I got over to what they call Tremantina in the middle part of the state, somewhere close to Tucumcari. I stopped there at a lady's house with a sign out front said ROOMS. I wanted to rent a room and clean myself up and get a good night's sleep. I got the room for a quarter. The next morning I got up and went out and here was two goats on top of my car. Their feet had gone through the roof of the touring car, and they were up there blatting their heads off with their legs hanging down inside the car.

We managed to lift the goats off of there, but they had torn my roof all to hell, it was nothing but rags. The old lady was very obliging and gave me some food to eat on my way, and she gave me my quarter back because she was sorry her goats had ruined my car roof.

On the touring car you could lay the top back like a roadster. So I laid the top back and traveled around without a roof. That was fine when the sun was shining, but without a roof and no side curtains—without a roof you couldn't put up side curtains—I was in trouble one day when between a little Mexican town and Las Vegas there come up this horrible thunderstorm.

The baby and I were getting beat to death with this big New Mexico hail. So I got out and slid under the car and laid there with the baby on top of me so the hail wouldn't beat on us. We were laying down under the car and trying to keep dry as we could, and pretty soon here comes the water running down the road under my back, ice cold. But I couldn't come out, I had to stay there holding the baby till the storm was over. Of course the seats were all wet, everything was a mess. But I got the car started—you had to crank them by hand in those days, you didn't have a starter—so I cranked it up and went back to Las Vegas. That was really an experience.

One day while I was running all over New Mexico to find a place to settle, I drove across the border over by Gallup and into Arizona and found myself in the Petrified Forest. Here was all these beautiful old pieces of log just laying around, petrified wood, a whole great field of them. They were so pretty I thought they must be worth something. Maybe I could sell them. I was pretty low on cash. So I loaded a whole bunch of them in the back of the car.

I was going up this washboardy road back toward Gallup when all of a sudden a big crash, and the car stopped, dust rising all over the place. The touring car had just a little thin board floor, the kind of board they used to make trunks out of, or the back wall of a buggy. Real thin little boards.

The floor had give way and fallen through and dropped all these rocks on the highway, and my car wouldn't clear them. It was hung up on all this petrified wood. I had to jack the car up to get the hind wheels over it and back on the ground so they could get some traction.

Well, I drove on from there, but down a ways there had been a wash across the highway from the rain. They had no bridges in those days, and I got stuck in this wash. I had no shovel with me. I had to take my frying pan and shovel up this sand and mud. Then I had to use my bed blanket under the wheels to get traction so I could get out of that arroyo. Right on the main highway. They didn't grade roads in those days. That's when I decided I'd better go back to Albuquerque.

Once back in Albuquerque I soon managed to buy another top for the car and put it on myself, so I never got caught out in the rain again.

5 | I LAND IN THE DUKE'S CITY

When I got to Albuquerque I had thirteen dollars and a quarter and this little kid not yet a year old. I looked around and finally went to a place up on Second Street that said APARTMENT FOR RENT. The place belonged to this Italian lady, Mrs. Bachechi. The Bachechis owned a lot of stuff around Albuquerque, very rich people. Her family built the KiMo Theater. These moving picture palaces were springing up all over the country in the twenties, some made to look Chinese, some like mosques. But the KiMo was unique. It was fashioned after Southwestern Indian pueblos.

After all the running around, Albuquerque looked better than any place else. I thought I had a chance of getting a job there. But I had no training, no education at all in the way of getting a job. Well, Mrs. Bachechi had seen me driving around town in the Model T. She was quite thrilled when I showed up at her door looking for a place to rent. She had a Packard sedan and she wanted to hire me for her chauffeur.

She gave me the apartment free and hired a maid to take care of my kid. I ate with her, too, in her dining room, and I got off pretty easy. She gave me a little spending money, not very much. Soon I was herding her all over town in her Packard sedan.

About this time I was having some female trouble after having the baby, and that's how I happened to go to this lady doctor, Dr. Evelyn Frisbee. Dr. Frisbee gave me good advice. She told me if I didn't want to have any more babies to keep my feet in a bucket. I told her there were lots of things I couldn't do if I kept my feet in a bucket. For one, you couldn't keep your feet in a bucket and ride a horse. I'd already set my mind on one day becoming a rancher.

She said, "That's all right. You can't do anything else, either, when you're straddling a horse."

Dr. Frisbee was a socially prominent person, but she befriended me, a nobody, when I was in a strange place among people I didn't know. She told me in spite of the hard times I'd gone through in Colorado, my lungs were healing. Whenever I was in need of advice I knew I could drop in on her. She was my doctor.

I needed to make more money, so when I wasn't chauffeuring Mrs. Bachechi I went out and looked around to see what I could find. I saw people working in their yards, planting and trimming and putting fertilizer on their lawns. I found out there was a big stockyard down in the South Valley. So I put some boards across the busted-out floor of the Model T, and I got several wash tubs, and I went down to the stockyard and filled them up with sheep manure and sold it to people as fertilizer for their yards. I charged them two bits a tub. It was a good thing cars were open then. Sheep manure is smellier than a hog pen in the rain.

Well, I was making a little change off that, and I also got a job at the Franciscan Hotel as a maid. I didn't know anything about maid's work. I didn't even know how to make up a bed the way they made them up professionally. I was surprised to find all these liquor bottles in the rooms. I didn't know about people partying that way, in hotel rooms, with liquor and all.

People would leave their tips there on the dresser. I gave all the tips to the boss at the desk. I didn't know you were supposed to keep them, and he never saw fit to enlighten me. I had to learn from my own experience, find out everything for myself.

Well, I hauled tubs of sheep manure, and I lived at Mrs. Bachechi's and drove her around in that Packard car, and I worked at the Franciscan hotel for a while, till Mrs. Bachechi told me to go ahead and quit. Life was looking up.

In Albuquerque in the early twenties they had women running the streetcars. There was one bus in town then, but they couldn't find a driver for that. So this guy from City Electric—City Electric owned the bus—who had seen me driving this Packard car around town, came up to Mrs. Bachechi's wanting to hire me to drive the city bus. It was such good pay—twenty-three dollars a week, that was a lot of money then—that I took the job and became the first woman bus driver in Albuquerque. I drove the bus from 1923 to 1927.

Once I had a good job, I didn't have time to run Mrs. Bachechi around town in the Packard, so I had to find another place to live. I set out to buy a little house on Eighth Street. It was actually a chicken coop. I guess it was about ten-by-twelve, something like that. That's when I found out that, if you were married, a woman had to have the husband's signature on everything. And of course that was not available. So I had to get shut of Parker.

Mother raised hell. She said there had never been a divorce in the family, and she didn't believe in divorces or separations and that kind of thing.

But I told her, Well, you don't have to live with him, and he had no way of supporting me or my baby, so therefore there was no point in my staying with him. He couldn't even make a living for himself. I think Mother wanted me married off as a way of taming me into what a woman at that time was supposed to be. Well, it wasn't going to work.

I went to an attorney and asked him what I should do about this situation. Turned out, a man, he didn't believe in divorce either. He said I could get a legal separation, and then I could do business in my own name.

So that's what I got, a legal separation. That freed me to go ahead and do what I wanted. And I guess it gave Parker plenty of rope to hang out and do any adultering he wished, he didn't have to look in the yellow pages for it.

So now I had my own chicken coop house. I deloused it and papered it on the inside with red building paper. We had a bed in there and a little wood stove with a cook stove top to it—that was our heat, me and the baby. It was just a little room of our own. The next-door neighbor took care of Anita while I was at work.

We were getting along pretty well there, but by and by as Anita got older—she was about three years old by then—it turned out to be very hard working and taking care of the baby too. So Mother told me to bring her back east and she would put her in this school where they took care of children twenty-four hours a day, five days a week. So I took Anita back east, another long train trip, when she was about four years old. Back in Pittsburgh Clifford took her to the school every Monday and left her till Friday night and went and picked her up again.

Then City Electric went out of business, and for a few years there wasn't any public transportation in Albuquerque. I thought I was surely going to starve. I had to find something else to do.

During my bus-driving days, I had gone to the Western School for Private Secretaries run by the Kelleher sisters. Whenever I had a chance to go to school, why I'd go—sometimes at night, maybe in the afternoon or my day off. The Kelleher sisters were very nice to me and let me come in any time I was able. They helped me out as much as they could, and that was a lot. I learned a little bit about bookkeeping, a little bit about typing, a little bit about everything they taught, but I certainly wasn't qualified for a secretarial job because I was only going to school in my off hours. I finally got a job checking in a grocery store. That didn't pay very much, about four dollars a week, but at least I was living.

6 | PARKER KIDNAPS ANITA

Then that bastard Parker stole Anita. My mother had been in touch with him and that's how he knew where the baby was. He was the father, so he was allowed to see her. He just went to the school and got her. I didn't know where he had taken her. For four years I tried everything I knew to find her. I didn't have any idea where she was or even if she was alive.

But in time I found out that this Bible Institute he had been going to studying ministry, being a good Christian outfit had sworn he was the only parent. He'd gotten a passport for her by saying her mother was dead. And the bastard had gone to Africa as a missionary and taken Anita with him. You hear a lot nowadays about a parent stealing off with a child to a foreign land, but back then there was a lot less of that kind of traveling.

I didn't know anything about writing letters or who to write them to or how to go about trying to get her back to the States. All I could do was bide my time and save up my money so I could go to Washington, D.C. When I thought I'd saved enough, I went back to Pittsburgh. This time I drove cross-country. There weren't any cross-country highways then. I had to make my way east by zigzagging on dirt section roads. At night I slept in the fields or in some farmer's yard.

In Missouri, somewhere near St. Louis, one of my axles broke. I managed to roll off the road into a field. It was late in the day, so when I spied some inviting-looking grass, soft and green, under big shade trees, I decided that would be my campground. I walked to the farmhouse to get permission, and the farm couple said I could camp out there. I couldn't do anything till the next day about the axle, so I bedded down in my blankets for the night.

I woke up real quick. I was being eaten alive by a murderous tribe of chiggers. I jumped up and ran to the farmhouse, and the woman took me to the barn and tore off my clothes and bathed me all over with kerosene. That killed the chiggers. I asked them how they managed to steer clear of the pests enough to tend their farm. They said they put flowers of sulfur in their shoes and it worked its way into their skin, and that kept the chiggers off.

They let me stay in their spare room that night. The farmer told me he had to go to St. Louis the next day and he would bring me back a new axle, which he did. We jacked up the car as best we could and installed it. Then I left out of there, but I'll never forget that adventure. Missouri is terrible for chiggers.

Somehow or other I finally got to Pittsburgh to some friends—an old man named Schwartz and his sister. Jake Haney, their half-brother, had a woodworking shop there. Jake and Miss Schwartz were in sympathy with me. By then my car needed repairs, so they put me in their old car and the three of us set out for Washington.

Jake's car was one of the first ever made. I don't know what kind it was. It ran with belts on a drive shaft. Every few miles you had to get out and sprinkle sand on the drive shaft to keep the belt from slipping. Something to do with the clutch.

Well, we finally get to Washington. Somehow I found the department that had to do with people carried off to foreign countries. The kidnapping became quite a case. Parker was ordered to get Anita back here, and he was told he couldn't come back to the States for eight years, else he would face a kidnapping charge.

But it was a couple of years before I had Anita with me again. She couldn't cross the ocean on a ship all by herself, she was just a little thing. But the government got after Parker till he finally shipped her back with some woman on the missionary station who was coming home.

All these things just happen in your life and you coast along till you learn how to deal with them.

Frances in front of the Model T Ford Touring
Car bought with one of her last Liberty Bonds
from World War I and converted into her first
camper with a cabinet for foodstuffs attached
to the body and the lid lowered as a worktable.
In this Model T she fled with nine-month-old
Anita over the Raton Pass to New Mexico,
1921. Photo courtesy of Sara Peck.

Frances standing on the motor of Albuquerque's first city bus with her uniform cap in hat in hand and her change belt around her waist, 1923. Photo courtesy Sara Peck.

Frances was one of the women hired by
City Electric as streetcar conductors, ca
1925. Photo Courtesy of Sara Peck.

The first three motorcycles
with sidecars of Frances's "Hurry
Up Delivery Service," ca 1930.
Photo courtesy of Sara Peck

Frances in front of her Studebaker
President Eight, ca. 1932.
Photo courtesy of Sara Peck.

Frances with husband Bob Martin in the
mid-1930s, at about age thirty-seven.
Photo courtesy of Dorothy Major.

Anita doing laundry in front of the cabins before the ranch house was built. Photo courtesy of Dorothy Major.

The back of the ranch house with
the water tank atop the milk shed,
Frances's daughter Anita saddling
the horse, and the car always kept
covered because the goats liked
to eat the rubber off the wiper
blades. The short gable covered the
screened back porch and the stairs
to the second-floor dormitory. The
generator was housed under the
milk shed, the storage batteries on
the back porch. The milk was run
through the cream separator in the
shed. After keeping what was
needed for the house, the surplus
was fed to the pigs. Butter was
churned as needed, and Frances's
husband Bob took cream and butter
to sell in Albuquerque. Photo
courtesy of Dorothy Major.

Frances on her way back to the ranch
house after a ride up the canyon with
friends. Photo courtesy of Dorothy Major.

Frances after a successful day of fishing in the upper
pond, with (right) her stepdaughter Darlene and (left)
her daughter Anita. Photo courtesy of Dorothy Major.

Frances driving the tractor and pulling the disker, rake, and other machinery, "getting it all done in one operation" with the help of hired man Frank, 1938. Photograph courtesy of Sara Peck.

Neighbors feasting at a barbecue and rodeo Frances held on the ranch. Photo courtesy of Dorothy Major.

A baby pig stealing milk from a cow, as the piglets did when a cow lay down or stood still enough for them. Photo courtesy of Dorothy Major.

Frances and her husband Bob with the chuck wagon on the Magdalena Driveway. Frances had added bowed ribs onto the truckbed to hold a tarp that provided some privacy and kept things dry. Photo courtesy of Dorothy Major.

Frances on Spur Ranch in front of
one of her cattle trucks, ca 1943.
Photo courtesy of Sara Peck.

Frances on her mare in Taos, 1960s.
Photo courtesy of Sally Whiteley.

Getting ready for a chicken dinner, Taos,
1960s. Photo courtesy of Sally Whiteley.

Frances and Hildegarde and Hildegarde's new calf
Esmeralda, Taos, 1960s. Photo courtesy of Sally Whiteley.

Frances with friend Marlon Brando, Taos,
mid-1970s. Photo courtesy of Janice Mars.

Frances in the Taos
landscape, 1972.
Photo courtesy of
Janice Mars.

Frances, age seventy-two, at her favorite
pastime. Photo courtesy of Dorothy Major.

Frances gardening in Taos at eighty.
Photo courtesy of Dorothy Major.

Frances with stepdaughter Dorothy Major in Truth or
Consequences at eighty-five. Photo courtesy of Dorothy Major.

Back in Albuquerque I decided to get in the rooming-house business. I rented a big old empty house, but I didn't have any money to buy furniture. So I went to a secondhand man, an old boy by the name of Logan. I never will forget him.

I told him what I wanted to do, and he said, "Anybody as ambitious as you are, I'm going to help you out. Take me down to this house and show me what you need. I've probably got enough stuff around here to furnish it up and get you started, and you can pay me off as you rent out your rooms."

So that's what I did. I took him down and showed him the house I'd rented and, sure enough, he dragged in all the furniture—beds and mattresses and tables and chairs—that I needed to start the rooming house.

Once I got it set up, I rented rooms to railroad men. They were just in there for maybe one or two nights a week—you know, the way railroad men come and go. Like, say, they were running from some place in Colorado to Gallup, whatever their run might be, and staying overnight in Albuquerque. They were no trouble. I didn't see very much of them. So that turned out all right. And in whatever spare time I had I roasted peanuts on the back porch of the boarding house and put them up in little packages attached to cards. I got businesses to carry them for sale on their counters.

So I had the rooming house going and the peanuts going while I was working at the grocery store. And I also worked one afternoon a week at an auction house. There I hit on an idea for another little business. I bought some of the things that went pretty cheap at the auction sales, then had an auction of my own. I rented a house and furnished it up with the stuff I bought out of the auction sales, because I thought people would pay more for the furniture from a house looked like somebody'd just moved out of and the furniture was being sold, than they would out of an auction house.

As it turned out that was true. After I paid off the auctioneer I made a little profit off of that business, too. And that worked out all right.

The next thing I did, I got into entertainment.

As I was growing up, my mother never allowed me to go to dances. I could only go to church and sing hymns. I guess she was trying to keep me from running the streets and being a whore, which I never had any inclination for anyway. She used to take me to all these concerts with old lady Schumann-Heink and that guy—what was his name? Caruso—and there I would have to set and listen to them screaming their heads off, couldn't understand a word. I was disgusted. Great big old fat thing setting up there yelling. I just got to where if anybody turned on classical music, and it starts going way up high and then all of a sudden dying out to practically nothing, why I feel like picking up that music box and crashing it on the floor.

But in spite of that, I'd always been musically inclined. I loved to sing. And since I had a pretty good blues voice, about this time I got a job evenings and weekends singing with Monty Blue and his orchestra. I dressed up in an evening dress and walked around among all these bald-headed men, singing the blues. These old guys would try to grab at me when I walked past them, and I'd pat them on the head.

Some nights I made as much as fifteen dollars. That was good money in those days.

Once I was making money singing I bought a saxophone and started taking saxophone lessons from this lady, Rose Jenkins, who taught piano and violin and other instruments. Rose Jenkins's husband was an arthritic person. All his joints had frozen. He couldn't move a joint in his body. If you pushed his head back, he feet came up, and if you pushed his feet down his head came up. Every joint in his body had solidified. Rose was having a hard time taking care of him and also making ends meet. So I finally moved in with her to help her take care of him, and that way got my saxophone lessons free.

Pretty soon I was singing with Monty Blue and also filling in playing B flat tenor sax with several little orchestras that came through Albuquerque. So the entertainment business was working out all right.

About this time this young guy Lindburgh was flying the mail out around here. Had this little two-wing airplane—not little to us then, but it'd seem mighty small now—and for five dollars he'd give you a flying lesson. Five dollars was a lot of money then, but I was kind of interested in this flying business, so I bought two flying lessons. That was all the lessons it took. I was a quick learner, and I learned flying wasn't for me. You were right out there in the great beyond, nothing over your head but sky. You had to wear goggles to protect your eyes. I didn't care for it. And that's held good to this day. I've flown when I had to, here and there. The last time I went up I took a bottle of bourbon along to help me get where I was going.

Along about here I got Anita back. While I worked at my jobs Rose looked after her. Anita was going to school and growing into a pretty girl. From a little thing, she talked about Africa and playing with the little black children. We had that in common—my playmates had been little black children too, down in Virginia. I knew Parker had kidnapped her to spite me, but he'd been a pretty good father to her while he had her. Now here she was, my daughter the world traveler.

While I was running the boarding house and singing with Monty Blue, I expanded into the used car business. I got acquainted with the Carborough Automobile Company when I bought a couple of cars from them that they advertised cheap. I fixed them up—repainted and reupholstered—and resold them for a little profit. So the Carborough Auto Company made me an offer: if I would rent a lot and sell used cars for them, they would furnish the used cars and pay me off in more used cars to sell for myself.

That sounded like a pretty good deal. I managed to get hold of this filling station that was for lease, a Sinclair station. The first thing you know, I've got five or six or, I don't know, a dozen or more of these old clunkers setting around the filling station with For Sale signs on their windshields. So that's how I got into the car business. Along with the rooming house and the peanuts and the auction sales and the entertainment business, I'm pumping gas and selling old cars.

I had an Indian and his wife there working for me, Pima Indians from Arizona. Dana was good at repairing and painting and fixing up the cars, and his wife was very good at upholstery. It was going right well when I heard about a big wholesale used-car sale going on in El Paso. I thought I could get a few better-class cars down there. Before I went I arranged to have them financed.

So I went to El Paso for the auction. I took Dana and his wife, and Rose Jenkins, and we figured we could pick up another driver down in El Paso, which we did.

I bought eight cars down there and we got them hooked up together, towing some of them, and started back to Albuquerque. We got up to Hot Springs with them—later they called it Truth or Consequences—when it started to storm. It got colder and colder, and finally the snow was really coming down. We managed to get as far as Nogal Canyon a little way out of Hot Springs, heading for Albuquerque, but we got stuck on the hill coming up out of the canyon.

Here we were with all these cars. Some would have run without being towed if we could have got them up that long slick hill. The trouble was, they didn't have any water in their radiators, and the temperature was dropping so fast that, even if we'd had water, which we didn't, we wouldn't dare get them started because we had no antifreeze. I drove back to Hot Springs and tried to buy antifreeze. There wasn't a gallon anywhere in the whole town. So there we were, stalled out in this snow storm in the middle of nowhere.

But I had this big car, a Studebaker President Eight. That Studebaker was a real automobile. You could've pulled a one-ton truck out of a hole with it. So I tied one of these cars to the Studebaker Eight and jerked it out of there and, sure enough, by fits and starts, got up the hill with it. Then I went back for the next one.

We were paddling around there—Rose and Dana's wife and I—in high heel shoes and fur coats, but we managed to get those cars up the hill one at a time by pushing and shoving and sliding around. We didn't get out of Nogal Canyon till around two o'clock in the morning. After that we didn't have any more trouble getting into Albuquerque. And I made some money off of those cars. The car business was turning out all right.

I was checking out groceries and singing with Monty Blue and playing B Flat tenor sax with little bands that came through Albuquerque, and renting out rooms to railroad men and running auctions and taking care of the automobile business, and then, when I saw the grocery store had a problem—it had no delivery service—I decided to start one up.

I went out and bought two motorcycles on credit and put boxes— side cars—on them and hired two boys to ride them. I called it The Hurry Up Delivery Service. The boys ran around to all the grocery stores and the drugstores and dry-goods stores and picked up their parcels and delivered them. And that worked out all right. I did pretty good at that.

But I had to have a place for the motorcycles. When I found a lot on Twelfth Street by Gold, in the middle of town, with a little trailer thing setting on it, I rented the place and parked the motorcycles there. But no need to let the little trailer just set there and go to waste. I used it to open up a hot-dog stand.

There wasn't that much opportunity in Albuquerque at that time. You had to have two or three things going to keep you busy. So it was just one thing after another that I got into. I soon had a number of these small little businesses going, and each one did better than the one before. But I soon discovered I couldn't be ten places at once. I needed help running things. Rose's husband finally got so bad Rose couldn't make enough money to keep him and herself too and have any left over for his medical attention. So his father living in El Paso took him down there and put him in a hospital. Then for a while Rose stayed in Albuquerque and helped me out with my several little businesses. She took care of the telephone for the delivery service and sold hamburgers and hot dogs and my roasted peanuts at the hot-dog stand.

But it wasn't long before Rose moved back to El Paso to be near her sick husband and live with her sister, who had been living alone in the big old family house after her father died. But taking care of this husband for so many years had broke Rose's health. She died soon after moving to El Paso. Rose Jenkins was a very nice person.

The next thing I did, I tried to barge into banking. When I learned the grocery store was about to sell out, thinking I'd handled enough money at the grocery store to qualify for a job as a teller, I took myself over to the bank. But I didn't know teller was the job I was applying for. I went in there like a dumb nut and asked the bank president, Jack Reynolds, for a job as a cashier.

I think he got a laugh out of that. There's a big difference between a cashier and a teller. The guts I had, going in there and asking the bank president for a cashier's job. But Jack Reynolds was a gentleman. He took the time to talk to me. Since he seemed interested, I told him something about my several little businesses. He asked me what I aimed to do with my life, and I told him I wanted to be a rancher if I could ever save up enough money to get a ranch.

At the end of the interview he said, "Well, fill out an application and we'll see what we can do."

About this time things in the financial markets were coming to a head. It was right at '29, and the stock market crashed. It was a big mess. I had to dispose of some of my holdings because I didn't know how I was going to keep everything going.

I sold out the motorcycle delivery service. By that time I had eight or ten motorcycles running around town. I sold out to a fellow who took it over and renamed it Merchants' Fast Delivery. Finally some New York Jewish fellow came along who had an idea. He bought the delivery service and eventually incorporated it out in California as the UPS. That's where UPS originated.

8 I I MARRY MY SECOND HUSBAND

While Rose and I were together, sometimes one of us or both of us had a date, and we'd all go out together. And I was friends with an Albuquerque couple in the sheet metal business, Louie and Helen Facaroli—they were Italians—and Louis and Helen sometimes took us out to a place called Silo's, out there in Tijeras Canyon, the only nightclub in that area at that time. Once or twice a month a bunch of us would go out there to dances. That's where I learned to dance. It was no problem, though at first I was stepping on everybody's feet.

And we used to go to the Crystal Palace, a bar on Second or Third, near Lead, a nice respectable place. You could go in there in the evenings and sit down at the booths and have a beer. And sometimes this very refined-looking gent would be sitting up at the bar. I wondered why he was always there alone. I was kind of interested, so I asked the Facarolis about him. They knew him quite well. They invited him to our table. That's how I met Bob Martin.

Bob and I started meeting there and having a drink or two. Like me he was a single parent. His wife had died and he had these two little girls. A Spanish girl came in the daytime to take care of them, and he stayed with them at night. Sometimes he sent them down to

El Paso to their maternal grandmother, his dead wife Alice's mother. Grandmother Van Eaton took care of them when Bob couldn't.

Anyhow, Bob Martin decided we ought to get married. He was a good-looking fellow, but I'd learned looks didn't mean a damn thing. Parker had been good-looking, too.

After my experience with the preacher I was totally turned off this marriage business. I told myself and I told Bob Martin I was through with that forever. But Bob kept after me. It'd be good for our kids, he said. Life was easier for a married woman, he said. He said the Lord decreed a woman ought to have a man and vice versa, not go through life alone but two-by-two. Finally I told myself the whole world couldn't be wrong and me right, so maybe I ought to give this marriage business another try.

But if it come to that I had a problem. I hadn't been giving any thought to it, but I was still a married woman. I'd never got a divorce from Parker, just a legal separation. In '32 I decided I'd better get a divorce so if I wanted to remarry I would have the privilege of doing so. I looked into the matter and found out Parker was back in the United States. He was up in Colorado, back at his mother's place in Timnath. So I served him with the papers. All these years he'd been married to me he had an excuse not to have to marry any of the women he ran around with. And being married to him might have been a guard rail that kept me out of trouble. I couldn't get out and do things I might otherwise have done.

Anyway, the last part of '32 or early '33, somewhere around there, I got a divorce from Parker. This time he didn't object. I was finally shut of him. And in '34 Bob Martin and I got married. Then I had his children, Darlene and Dorothy, to raise Anita with instead of raising her all by herself. So now I'm Frances Martin.

We lived in a big house on Silver Street in Old Town. The house had a dumb waiter, and the kids played with it endlessly, sending things up and down. I was still working on the cars. I had a bunch of them in the yard. And though they were young, Darlene and Anita worked in the hot dog and hamburger stand with occasional help from me. We sold hamburgers for fifteen cents, and if sometimes a tourist ordered a steak, why, one of us would run out the back door to the butcher on the corner, then run back and throw it on the grill.

Bob had been drinking pretty heavy before I married him, when he lived alone, and he continued to drink for quite some time after we were together. After he had the DT's two or three times, I determined to do something about it. I went to Dr. Frisbee and asked her opinion of the drying-out cures I'd heard about in California. She told me some of these cures were pretty violent. "He might die if you take him out there," she said, "but he'll die for sure if you don't."

"Well," I said, "He's no good to himself or anybody else the shape he's in."

When finally it looked like it could kill him, I drove him out to California to a place recommended to me by people who'd been there.

I had a time with Bob on the drive out. He was wilder than a mule with a burr under his tail, having DT's again. I often had to pull off the highway and calm him down, but I finally managed to get him to California. I left him there at the clinic and drove back home to Albuquerque and the kids.

I never knew what all went on at the clinic. The treatment lasted for two weeks. When I went back to get Bob, I told the clinic doctor all his friends drank, and everybody I knew was drinking, and I asked him whether or not I should keep liquor around the house.

The doctor said, "Do as you like. He's not going to want it."

The doctor was right. Bob never drank any liquor after that. That was the end of his drinking. He just quit, period.

After he was cured he got pretty intolerant of drinking. He'd pick up a glass and smell it, and if it had liquor in it he would dash it down and break it. He broke glasses all over the house.

9 I I REALIZE MY BIG AMBITION

At the time of the crash in 1929 some of the Albuquerque banks went broke, and The First National was one of them. Jack Reynolds, the bank president I'd stupidly asked for a cashier's job, was Bob's brother-in-law. His wife Mabel and Bob's first wife Alice were sisters. When Jack came by the house one day I thought he was looking for Bob but turned out he was looking for me.

"You once told me you'd like to go into ranching," he said. "Do you still aspire to be a rancher?"

I said yes, I did.

"Well," he said, "I've got two ranches down in Catron County that we've had to foreclose on."

He explained that as one of the officials in the bank, he had to turn some of the frozen assets into liquid assets. Some kind of business with banking law I didn't know anything about. That's how it happened that Jack Reynolds turned the running of two ranches, Spur Ranch and Centerfire, over to me.

He told me, "If you make any money off them, I want half the proceeds over and above your expenses, but don't run up any debts."

So Bob and I talked it over, then I went down to Catron County and took over these two ranches.

There was no stock on the ranches when I got them, but it didn't take me long to build up a herd. In the middle of the Great Depression people didn't have any cash money. So I hauled down to Catron County forty of the old cars that Carborough had given me in payment for selling cars for them.

Then as now, everybody wanted a car. These Mormons down at Luna showed up on horseback leading cows and calves to trade for an old car with the battery down and the tires flat. Then they showed up again the next day with a pump and an old battery and got the car started up and drove it home.

Pretty soon I'd traded all the cars for cows. That's how I stocked the ranches. I sent to A&M for pamphlets on stock raising, and I got the ranches up and going. They were pretty big ranches. Including the forest permits and state permits, they were around thirty-six sections. A section is about 640 acres, or one square mile. So the ranches all together were over 18,000 acres, about thirty-six square miles.

That first year I lived in one of the one-room shacks at the base of the hill on Centerfire. Rose and Frank, the hired hand and his wife, lived in the other. Bob was tied down with his job in Albuquerque. He was associated with the Newlander Mill and Lumber Company in Albuquerque. They made window and door sashes and other fine cabinetry. Newlander later made doors and cabinets for the Lab in Los Alamos. They'd give out only part of a blueprint at a time, so you never really knew what you were working on. It was all top secret. At that time Bob handled the finances for the company, but later on he bought the company and managed it. Anyway, he was busy with Newlander but he got out to the ranch on weekends.

In the winter the kids lived with him in Albuquerque and went to school, but Anita and his two girls spent the summers out on the ranch with me. On the ranches we pretty much lived outdoors. But the shack had bunk beds and a wood stove for heating and cooking, and that first summer when the kids came out we all cooked and slept in there.

The ranches were about seventeen or eighteen miles northeast of Luna, which was our post office. The post office was also the country store where I bought staples and canned goods and all kinds of general merchandise you need around a ranch. We made the trip once a week for mail and supplies. Unless a cowboy from a neighboring ranch stopped by on horseback looking for stock, that was the only time we saw other people.

After the first year, I hired help from around there and got the ranch house built on a hill overlooking the spread, and I also built a log house back from the crest for Rose and Frank. I planned the house myself. It had a big main room with a huge stone fireplace at one end, which was our source of heat. It had a concrete hearth sunken for safety in case a log rolled out. Three bedrooms and the kitchen opened off the back of this big main room, and a screened porch stretched all across the front.

The eat-in kitchen had a big sink and counter and a wood stove with a water tank. Just off the kitchen was a pantry and a bathroom, and back of that another screened porch with steps leading up to the girls' dormitory, a big open loft with gables overlooking the valley. The stock wasn't penned up, so the cows scattered all over the grassland. From the ranch house on the hill you could look out and see all the livestock grazing.

About this time, Mrs. Mabry—Governor Mabry was in office here at that time, and she had something to do with delinquent children—Mrs. Mabry sent two boys out to the ranch. Their mother had lost her mind during her change of life and couldn't take care of the kids. Stanley and Ernest were about twelve or thirteen years old, around the age of the girls. I put Stanley and Earnest in one of the bedrooms downstairs. They were a big help around the place.

The ranch road—north from Horse Springs or south from Luna and Reserve, the county seat—was nothing but a two-rut track with high centers. It wound through a high mesa landscape, a terrain of valleys and low grassy hills with very few trees. The road was clay and pretty slick, with spots of caliche, which was even slicker. After a rain it was full of mud holes. You had to keep up your speed or get stuck.

Road maintenance was just part of life on the ranch. We got stuck so often we carried shovels and everything else in the truck that could help us get out. I always drove a Dodge pickup because it had a high clearance and was a reliable work horse.

When we got stuck we dug out with the shovels and cut rabbit brush or greasewood to shove under the wheels for traction. We had to get behind those spinning wheels and push. If we got stuck on our way to Luna, we ended up in town, all five kids and I, covered head to foot with mud. Centerfire was at the end of the road, so on our way home, a few miles off the blacktop and we were on our own for that last, worst stretch. About a quarter mile from the ranch house, the track went through a broad arroyo that meant trouble in dry weather and hell in wet. So finally, if it looked like rain and we had to go to town, we drove the truck to the other side of the arroyo and left it there, then hiked back to the house. That way we knew we could get out if we had to.

On the house side of the arroyo the road climbed up a low hill. Once you made the top, you could see the ranch spread out in the valley below and, across the valley, the ranch house overlooking it from atop another hill.

The driveway up to the house circled to the back yard where there were two big ponderosa pines. Everybody who came around parked under them to get out of the sun. So the kitchen door was really our entry. Visitors complained when the baby goats explored the tops and hoods of their cars and ate their windshield wipers. But those kids were the children's pets. They got a lot of attention, and they were smart. They learned to open the back porch door, so sometimes we'd hear the patter of twenty little feet and five baby goats would come through the kitchen and into the main room. We also had a nanny and a billy. My stepdaughter Dorothy made some harness and trained the billy to pull a wagon.

We got our drinking water from a spring down the hill. The first couple of years we had to carry our water up the hill in buckets, quite a chore on wash days. But once I built a water tower out of cedar on top of hill in back of the house, we pumped water up from the spring to fill the tank. From there it was gravity feed to the house. In time I put a gasoline engine under the water tower to power a generator so we could have electricity. That meant a radio, and music!

I taught the youngsters how to call the chickens and hogs back to the house in the evening at feeding time. You'd see them grazing a mile away lift their heads and listen, then at the second call start running home. The kids loved that. All the animals had names. We knew them as individuals.

I wasn't long on the ranch before I got a contract with Borden Company in El Paso to raise heifers, young cows, for them. Bordens trucked the heifers to the ranch as soon as they were weaned from the mother cows. That way the dairy, instead of the calves, got the milk. Then when the heifers grew up and dropped their first calves and their milk was in, Bordens came and got them and trucked them back to El Paso. They let me keep the calves. That way the dairy got all the milk.

They not only gave me the calves, they paid me eight cents a pound for all the gain I had put on the heifers. When they brought them to me they were little calves, and by the time they came and got them they were cows that had already birthed and were giving milk, so there was considerable weight difference. I made good money off that deal.

Of course they were all bred by my white-face bull. That made them half dairy cattle and half white face. Our cattle—Holsteins and Jerseys and half-Herefords—were so many different colors the Mormons in the community took to calling the place The Rainbow Ranch.

The long lane in to the house was fenced off with barb wire from lush green meadows good for grazing, on one side the horse pasture and on the other a grassy bog full of natural springs. People in the neighborhood told me I couldn't run cattle there because I'd lose half of them in that bog. It was pretty good size, maybe six or eight acres.

Sure enough, now and then a cow got trapped. We'd try prying it free, twisting its tail to encourage it to give us a little help. If that didn't work we brought down a horse to pull it out. I thought I'd better cure this situation, so I climbed on the tractor and gouged out a pond about a quarter mile above the upper end of the draw that ran into the bog. The pond trapped some of the water and kept it from running into the bog. Enough water collected to make a small lake with a depth of about eight feet. It soon became a watering hole for the cattle and horses, a place for ducks to congregate, and a schooling ground where the mother ducks and geese taught their babies to swim. Before I ran water to the house, this was where everybody had a bath once a week. And it made a good swimming hole. I built a barrel raft so the kids could dive and sun bathe. And after I stocked the pond with trout, I loved to fish in it.

The next improvement meant taking the bulldozer down and damming up the far lower end of the bog. Here I made a second lake, this one pretty shallow. I dragged logs over and hauled dirt to dump on top of them. Then I hauled more logs and covered them with more dirt till I had a dam there you could ride across. Water backed up till I had about four feet of depth in this lower pond.

People said I ought to be draining that bog instead of damming it up, but after I built the ponds I never lost any cows in there, never got but one cow stuck, and that was before the water collected very deep. After enough water backed up and covered the bog, they didn't try to wade out in it. They just went to the edge and drank.

This second lake also provided water for the animals and wildlife as well as another fishing hole I stocked with bass and trout. It spread out wide, and the hills coming down looked like giants sitting there on the shore with their knees up and their feet in the water.

In time Frank and I built an ice house out of two-by-twelve lumber into the side of the hill below the house. The ice house had two rooms. We cut our ice from the pond in winter and stored the blocks, covered with sawdust, in the back room built into the hill, and we kept our food in the front room, our cold storage locker. We could store our meat there throughout the summer. Whenever we wanted to cook some of it, we had a time cleaning off all the sawdust.

One year I decided to raise some turkeys for the Albuquerque market. I built a turkey house complete with roosts and ordered several hundred turkey chicks. At twilight we had to go out to the pen and put each one of the dumb little things on the roosts by hand until they finally learned to get up there by themselves. Otherwise they roosted on top of one another and some on the bottom were smothered to death. We had to pluck a lot of feathers before we got them to market.

I also bought boxes of baby chicks to raise. They weren't near the trouble the turkeys were. I raised them for our table and for eggs to market in Luna when I went in for supplies.

I also sold cream and butter in Luna. And I put some of the eggs into stone crocks filled with a liquid that sealed the pores in the shells. That way I saved the eggs and had plenty for the ranch when the hens weren't laying.

Because of the altitude and the open landscape, electrical storms can be very dangerous in that part of New Mexico. It was pleasant to have the house on top of a hill, shaded by those big trees, where it caught the breeze, but the hilltop and the trees made the house vulnerable to lightning strikes. One night lightning came down the chimney and knocked Darlene clear across the kitchen into the living room. Scared her pretty bad. Many's the time I grabbed the kids out of bed in the middle of the night when a storm came up. I hustled them outside and put them in the truck and backed the truck down the hill to where we'd all be safe in case one of the pines got hit. Sometimes we just about spent the night in the truck.

One evening during a cloudburst with lots of lightning, we stood helpless on the front porch and watched the water rise across the lower cienega till it forced the cattle onto higher ground at a fence corner way across the valley. The storm kept up till late, but whenever lightning lit up the landscape we could see what was happening.

One by one the cows swam across to safety till only one old cow we called Grandma was left stranded with her calf. Old Grandma kept backing up and up into the fence corner till she couldn't back up any more. She was trapped there with the fence behind her and the water in front of her.

Then in the next lightning flash we saw Old Grandma swimming, but no calf anywhere. We could see she was being carried downstream, and we knew the calf had been carried away and drowned.

We watched till finally she reached the shallows where she could touch bottom. And when she walked out of the water, lo and behold, beside her was her calf. She had put it on her upstream side where the force of the water kept it plastered against her as she swam. It was a relief to see they were both safe. Every loss is substantial when you're operating on a shoestring, and the kids were attached to every animal on the place.

Except for Frank, the youngsters were my only help on the ranches. They milked the dairy cows I raised for our own cream and milk and butter, then took the milk to the water-tower shed and ran it through the separator to get the cream out. I saved the cream in stone crocks till it was ready to be churned for butter. They also weeded the garden, fed the stock, and cleaned the pens. After we cut and dried the hay in the fields, they helped load it onto the truck. That meant walking along the windrows with pitch forks and tossing it onto the truckbed. Or if I had a baler come in, they helped buck the bales onto the truck and then unloaded and stacked them back at the corral. At the end of the day we were all bone tired and itchy all over from the hay in our clothes.

The kids all got along pretty well, but one day Stanley and Dorothy got in a fight down in the corral and she came in with tears rolling down her face.

I asked her who won the fight and she said, "I did."

"Well then," I said, "what are you crying about?"

She said she hadn't won fair because she was taller than Stanley and she could beat him up all over but he couldn't land a blow much higher than her waist. I had a laugh out of that, but Dorothy didn't think it was funny.

The place was pretty quiet in the winter, when the kids went back to Albuquerque and lived with Bob and went to school, but in the summer they invited all their friends out to the ranch. Then the house looked like a beehive, always full of people, kids running back and forth. We never had any of that stepmother business. I treated the kids alike, made no difference among them. If one of them got something, they all got the same thing or the equivalent.

In the summertime Grandmother Van Eaton came out to the ranch from her home in El Paso. She was pretty crippled up with arthritis and she couldn't get around too well, but when I was out working on the ranch she did what she could around the house. She was very pleasant to get along with. She never complained about anything. Now and again she got after me for working the children too hard, but I'd worked hard all my life, it was natural to me, and I believed in teaching them how to do everything. Grandmother Van Eaton was a wonderful old lady.

Sometimes I loaded the kids up in the back of the truck and took them to dances over in Reserve and Luna. We always had a good time at the dances. They were held at the school house, and the musicians were locals. All the women seemed to be pregnant or have a baby hanging on their breast nursing, so there were always plenty of men to dance with. These old cowboys were dancing fools. They did what I guess was the two-step, herding their partners around in a circle on the dance floor, and they always had a bottle stashed outside. I slipped out now and then and had a nip with them.

One night we came home about midnight after a storm. When we got to that bad arroyo, we saw the storm had washed it even deeper. I thought maybe we could get across at a place where the dip was shallow, so we tried it and got stuck.

I kept some horses in a trap—a small fenced pasture where you keep your saddle horses so they're handy and easy to catch. I sent Stanley over to the trap to catch a couple of horses and bring them back with ropes to help pull the pickup out of the arroyo.

Pretty soon he comes back saying he can't catch the horses. I asked him why not. He said, "Ever time I run after them they run away from me." He'd gone after them with the flashlight, and the flashlight had spooked the horses. By the time we broke off enough rabbit brush and stuffed it in under the tires and finally got out of there, our dance clothes weren't going to any more dances.

We always dressed up for those dances, but it was on the ranches that I learned to wear pants. None of the women around there ever put on pants, I was the only one. I had to be on a horse most of the time, and it had come to my attention that every time I hired a man to do any work on the place, he spent a lot of time watching me crawl on the tractor with a dress on. I wasn't going to pay a man to stand around eyeing my legs. Once I put on pants, I've never taken them off.

My mother didn't have much truck with pants. One time I brought her out to the ranches. She visited for about a month. I don't know if she liked it or not. I saw her again in '36 or '37. I went back east, took the children on a train trip to Atlantic City—Darlene, Dorothy, and Anita—and I stopped and saw Mother at that time. That was the last time I saw her.

10 | RUNNING TWO RANCHES

Along with raising our own stock and the Borden cows, I got into raising Duroc Jersey hogs. Durocs are huge animals. One old Duroc boar, Jerry, was big enough to ride, and the sows weren't much littler. One time by mistake Jerry got put in with the breeding sows. He was in hog heaven. We like to never got him out of there. He was pretty mean, and so big he was dangerous. For safety's sake we finally had to catch him and saw off his tusks. The hogs were pretty prolific, so I had quite a few.

One day when I'd gone into Albuquerque to pick up a couple thousand pounds of hog feed, I had another bad experience with that arroyo. I was driving in to the ranch before I realized I'd never get down in that arroyo and out the other side with that load. So I parked the truck and walked in to the corrals and gathered up a string of horses and took them out to the arroyo.

I loaded two sacks of hog feed on each horse, and I had packed about six horses and started back to the house when the storm that had been brewing burst out in full force. Just as I came over the crest of the hill, lightning struck a tree right in front of me and knocked down the horse I was riding. The horses I was leading panicked and broke loose and bucked off their packs.

When I picked myself up, I had grain scattered all over the hill. There was no way to gather it to take to the hogs. But if you can't take the mountain to Mohammed, you can sure take Mohammed to the mountain. I rounded up the horses and got them corralled, and then gathered up the hogs and herded them over to the feed. I didn't have to feed those hogs for some time after that.

A little later on a flash flood made the arroyo completely impassable. I finally had to deal with the situation. I threw an earth-and-log ford across it up to about half its depth. Finally the thing was navigable.

Below the shallow pond and the second dam, the ranch land turned arid with a lot of caliche and grew almost nothing. Farther down, toward the end of Centerfire, was a meadow with an Indian ruin on a low hill. The signs of a pit house ruin are usually shards and arrowheads scattered around the surface, and maybe a *mano* or two—the hand-held grinding stones—or a piece of a *metate,* the bigger base stone, shaped like a saddle in the road, that they did their grinding on.

Another sign you'll often find is a prairie dog community on top of a pit house ruin, because the sunken underground dug-out, filled over time with dirt and debris, makes it easy for the prairie dogs to dig their tunnels. You always find those old pit house ruins on low hills over a draw that gets some seasonal run-off, where those early people could cultivate a little corn. Below our ruin was a rocky, almost box canyon with a spring and running stream where they must have got their drinking water. And whenever they needed to, they could carry it from the stream to their cornfield in the pots and watertight baskets the women made. It was through this canyon that we moved the cattle from Centerfire, the summer range, down to the winter range at Spur Ranch.

Spur Ranch had no irrigation except for one small parcel of about 40 acres where a former owner had planted some alfalfa. It wasn't very productive. The alfalfa was sparse and thin. I watered it and kept it going for a year or two before I finally gave up and plowed it under. Then I disced those fields and planted wheat and rye and squaw corn. I let the crops grow untouched in the summertime so I would have them for winter pasture. I also planted 35 or 40 acres of Jerusalem artichokes, which are very good feed for livestock as well as humans.

In the summer I kept all the stock at the upper ranch because Centerfire with its hills and valleys was all grazing land, but in winter I brought the herd down to Spur Ranch because it had about five hundred acres in a cultivatable valley where I had all that winter feed. I moved between the ranches with the seasons.

When the sows were nursing piglets, the kids and I went rabbit hunting at night. I drove and the kids stood in the back of the truck with rifles and shot rabbits when they froze in the headlights. We hunted rabbits because they multiplied so fast they ate the grass needed for the livestock, and we fed the carcasses to the sows to keep them from eating their piglets. That worked. We saved most of the baby pigs. The piglets were cute running free all over the place.

One summer our cows started producing a lot less milk. I thought the kids were getting careless and letting the calves in to their mothers. I gave them hell about it. But even after I made sure the calves were kept apart, the cows still gave lots less milk.

I couldn't figure out what was going on till I came in the corral late one night and caught the culprits in the act. After the cows lay down at night, the baby pigs were going over and nuzzling up and nursing to their hearts' content.

Along with the calves Borden let me keep, I made trips to the dairies in Albuquerque and bought their one- and two-day-old calves, paying anywhere from one to three dollars apiece for them. These dairies, like Bordens, wanted to get rid of the calves so they'd have the mothers' milk. I took the babies to the ranch, and the kids bottle-fed them.

Raising the calves was a tricky business. Sometimes we were lucky enough to find one of our own Hereford mothers who would take on a second calf besides her own, and sometimes one of the cows who'd lost her own calf was willing to take on an orphan.

But weaned so young and deprived of their mother's milk, which is very health-giving, the babies often got severe diarrhea, or scours. When that happened I mixed a medicine in the bottled milk, and the children fed them by letting them suck on their fingers while the milk preparation flowed into their mouths from the bottles, so the baby calves thought they were nursing. We lost some of the little calves, but we saved most of them to grow up on the ranch.

Frank and I built a cattle chute to run cattle through at branding time. We made the branding fire inside the corral, one iron heating up while we used the other. The kids roped the calves and threw them and tied them and held them while Frank and I castrated and medicated and vaccinated and branded and dehorned. We sold the bull calves as yearlings, but we kept the females to add to the ranch stock.

We worked so hard every day we didn't need much entertainment before falling in bed at night. Sometimes we played cards, and we got in a lot of reading. I enjoyed being read to. Whenever we had to drive to Albuquerque or El Paso, I had one of the girls read aloud to pass the time. And Anita and I sang. I taught her spirituals from my childhood days in the tobacco sheds, and blues songs from my days with Monty Blue. Anita inherited my voice.

For seeding and plowing I kept the caterpillar, the big T-20 International Crawler tractor, at Spur Ranch. Behind it I hitched on my twelve foot disc, the tandem disc, and the clod buster, and finally the harrow and the drill. Then I took off down through the field plowing and planting at the same time, getting it all done in one operation.

One day as I was going along, a big rock got caught in the drill. I throttled down the tractor so it was moving real slow, and jumped off and ran back to try to get this rock out of the drill. All of a sudden the throttle slipped and the tractor started going faster and faster, heading down toward the creek bank. And there went all my expensive machinery.

I ran like hell and jumped on just before it got to the creek, and saved the equipment. If the tractor had gone over the twenty-foot drop, I'd've lost it all.

I wasn't usually careless, but that day I'd started out upset. I always set out to get my work done early in the morning because we had a very short season. You only had a few days to get your seeding in. The night before, Bob had come out to the ranch and brought with him some company from Albuquerque. And Bob and Company were standing around not doing anything, just watching me fill the drill with seed and getting ready to take off. I saw they were waiting for me come back in and cook breakfast for them. Well, I wasn't going to do it. I had work to do. They could cook breakfast for themselves.

This smart gal friend of Bob's spoke up and said, "Come on, Bob, the lady has her plowing. We're just taking up her time."

The way she said that burned me up. I was mad at Bob for bringing her out. Mad at the whole outfit, I climbed on the tractor and worked all day. Late afternoon when I got off the tractor I didn't even go to the house. I got in my pickup and went to Uncle Bill's over at Reserve. I stayed there at the bar until nine or ten o'clock that night. When I came home the visitors were gone.

11 I WHISKEY-MAKING AND THE BISHOP'S VISIT

All of us living out in that country had a hard time buying good liquor. Traders made you buy worthless stuff before they'd sell you one bottle of good whiskey. If I wanted good liquor on hand for the cowboys and hunters and other visitors to the ranch, I had to drive down to Juarez to buy it. One fall after the kids were back in Albuquerque going to school, this guy Sam, who was digging a well for me, decided we'd make our own.

Whiskey has to be made in winter because you have to pack the coils in ice to cool them, and of course you had to get the ice off the ponds after they'd frozen over. You get your liquor from the distilled steam off the fermented stuff. Rationing was still going on because of the war, but as a rancher I could get all the sugar I wanted with my gasoline stamps.

Sam had a still and he loaded it up and brought it down to Spur Ranch. We put the still in a back room of the ranch house, and he got some corn chops working to make the sour mash.

The still was going *barooom barooom barooom* when Sam looked out the window and yelled, "Oh God, here comes the bishop! What'll we do?"

It was the Mormon bishop from Luna ambling up the hill on his horse. Whenever it got too late for people to make it home at night, why, they just stayed over at somebody's house. And it was too late for the bishop to make it back over the mountain to Luna.

We couldn't stop the contraption and it was making a hell of a racket. I had to think fast. I told Sam I'd go into my room and get the radio going full blast, and he could get the bishop into a pitch game outside my bedroom door close to the fireplace to get the full benefit of the noise.

I turned on the radio and prayed the batteries wouldn't run down, and Sam got the bishop into a game while I kept running in and out the back door, bringing more wood to put under the still.

After a while the bishop said, "Doesn't that woman ever turn that radio down?"

Sam said, "No! I've been here a week working on that well and I never yet got any sleep. She keeps it going like that day and night."

I doubt the bishop got much sleep either. The whiskey never finished till three in the morning, and he got out of there before sun-up. So we managed to get by without the bishop learning we were making liquor.

At daylight Sam sent me into Magdalena, a seventy-mile round trip, to get some oak kegs to put the whisky in and let it age. When I brought them back to the ranch, he said, "Th'ow some gasoline in them and th'ow in a match. That'll char the barrels."

I did as he directed, and I really charred those kegs. There was nothing left but the hoops. So back I went to Magdalena for more barrels—another seventy miles—and we charred them all over again, with less gasoline this time. We put the kegs in the attic to let the whiskey age. When finally we tasted it, I spit the stuff out on the floor and had a coughing fit.

"God, Sam," I said, "this stuff tastes terrible."

Sam said it was only about 120 proof. He drank that whiskey but I never did.

When a bakery burned in Socorro, Sam got the notion to try it again. We had all the corn we needed, so I went down and got about fifteen hundred pounds of that damaged sugar from the bakery fire. This time we put the still out in a bunkhouse. I wasn't going to have the stuff in the house any more.

Sam knew all about making whiskey, but about this time his wife took sick. He had to go home to look after her and wouldn't be there to run off the whiskey when it was ready. So he got this guy Rex and his wife to come over and finish the job.

Rex was a former bootlegger. He knew what he was doing when it came to making whiskey. But Rex and his wife got careless about watching the still. The bunkhouse caught fire and burned down, Sam's still burned up, and melted sugar ran like a lava flow down the yard to the irrigation ditch.

I turned the hogs out and they made short work of the sugar flow before the insurance people got their man out. And that was the end of my whiskey-making.

One thing I liked about ranch life, it was a very self-sufficient operation. You supplied all your needs except for white flour and sugar and salt, little else. Of course nowadays things have changed. Most ranchers buy everything out of a store. They don't even put in a garden. The only thing they raise at home is meat.

But I raised practically everything we ate. I planted a big garden and the kids helped take care of it. I canned green beans and peas and corn and everything I raised in the garden. And I had enough to get me through the year and also to feed Bob and the kids in town all winter.

The hogs and cattle were the money crop, too valuable to eat. For meat we ate squirrel or rabbit that the kids shot and brought home. And sometimes I'd go out and kill game. Though sport hunting was only legal in season, venison and antelope provided a lot of our meat on the ranch. I always fed the game wardens out-of-season meats when they came though, telling them it was beef. They always complemented me on the good beef dinner. They knew it was a lie, but they also knew the hunting on the ranch was only for food, not sport. I knew how to cook wild game so it was delicious.

Now and then to vary our diet I butchered a hog. Frank slit its throat and we roped the hind feet together and hoisted it up with a block and tackle to hang from a tree limb till it was bled. Then we built a fire under it and boiled water in a fifty-gallon barrel and lowered the carcass in the barrel for a few minutes to loosen the hair so we could scrape it off the hide. We butchered it up into hams and chops and rashers of bacon and stored it in the ice house.

I smoked some of the hams. I also made head cheese and ground up and seasoned some of the meat for sausage, which we stuffed into the cleaned-out intestines. I put the sausage down packed in lard in fruit jars, and it kept just like it was fresh.

For firewood we took periodic excursions into the forest to gather up dead trees. I rigged up an old automobile engine with a wide belt and a big saw blade, and cut the trees to lengths that could be split with a double-bit ax for the wood stove and the fireplace. One of the kids' chores was to keep the woodbox by the kitchen stove filled.

The stove was big, with lots of cooking space on top. I let beans simmer there all day. And by controlling the wood fire I could bake our breads.

12 | GETTING ALONG WITH THE NEIGHBORS

All the ranchers around there had long since decided this woman at Centerfire was plumb nuts, raising dairy calves and hogs and chickens and goats and turkeys instead of just beef, which they considered was the business of ranchers. But gradually they began to warm to the idea of having pork on their table. They began to trade purebred Herefords for my Duroc hogs. And once they saw I had plenty of milk and butter and cream from our mixed Jerseys and Holsteins and Guernsey cows, they started trading for those, too.

One summer I invited all the neighboring ranchers over for a barbeque and rodeo. I dug a pit and roasted a pig, and the women brought salads and breads and covered dishes and desserts. And in the makeshift corral Frank and I had built with a chute for the stock, the cowboys competed in roping and riding contests. I also had a calf-roping event for the kids. Everybody seemed to have a real good time.

But sometimes on the ranch I had trouble with my neighbors, probably because I was a woman out there ranching. Some of the men didn't think a woman was up to the job, and that led them to try a few tricks. After I got the contract with the Borden Company, occasionally some of the good-grade dairy heifers came up missing. So I made it a habit to round up the Borden stock and get a count on them at least once a week.

One time I came up four head short. I couldn't find them anywhere, and I couldn't find their bodies, so I knew they weren't dead. I thought maybe they had gotten in somebody else's pasture, though that wasn't likely because they weren't the kind of stock to break out and stray too far from home.

For two weeks I looked everywhere for these heifers. Finally I rode up a narrow little canyon on the side of Spur Ranch with a stream running through it that led over to Luna. I went up there about a quarter of a mile and heard this bellering. I kept going and found the heifers. Somebody had built a pole corral and had them penned. The ground was strewn with hay. Whoever it was had been bringing hay down there and feeding them. I just let them out of the corral and set the corral on fire, just burned the bastard up, and took the heifers back to the ranch.

I guess the rustlers thought they'd keep them there till I'd given up on ever finding them, then rebrand them and take them over as theirs. Well, they knew I'd found them whenever they saw the corral burned, but nobody ever said anything about it.

Spur Ranch and Centerfire weren't adjoining. One of my neighbors, a guy by the name of Hulsey, had a forest permit bordering on both ranches. Part of his place ran between them, touching on both. I had trouble with his stock getting in the Spur Ranch fields in the summertime and eating up the crops I was growing there for my winter feed.

Two or three times I found Hulsey's cattle in there and drove them out. And each time, I checked his fence line up a ways from the field and found the wire taken down from the posts, and logs and rocks laid on it to hold it down so the cattle could walk over it into my planted fields.

Every time it happened I rode by Hulsey's house and told him his cattle were getting into Spur Ranch and I wanted him to keep them out. And every time he just told me I had to fix the fence. I said I'd fixed the fence several times, and somebody kept taking it off the posts and putting it on the ground and laying weights on it, and I was fed up with that business. He said he didn't know who was doing it and he couldn't do anything about it.

The next time my fence was laid down and weighted with rocks and his cows were in my fields, I turned the gate on the irrigation ditch and let water onto the alfalfa. Then I got on my horse and rode over to his house.

He was sitting on the porch, had a horse tied up to the hitching poles out front like maybe he'd just got home.

I said, "Guess what, your cattle are in my Spur Ranch fields again."

He said, "Well, I can't keep them out of there. What're you going to do about it?"

I said, "I just turned the water on the alfalfa and there's about twenty-five head of your cattle in there grazing their fill."

Well, Hulsey jumped up like he'd been bit and ran in the house and grabbed up a kitchen knife and flew off his porch onto his horse without touching foot to ground and headed toward my field at a dead run. Eating green alfalfa wet will bloat a cow and kill it if the bloating isn't relieved in time with a knife.

That should have been the end of my troubles with Hulsey, but it wasn't. At the lower end of the upper ranch, Centerfire, I had eighty or one hundred acres of meadow land along both sides of the stream. I planted these acres with winter wheat and winter rye for spring pasture for my cows that were going to calve. They do better on green pasture when they're calving.

The winter wheat was doing well. I had a real good crop. But when I moved my cattle up there in the spring, here were some of Hulsey's cows. He had about forty head in there, in what we called the Luna Flats.

When I checked at the gate it was clear what had happened. I found fresh tracks of cattle and horses and roping boots, one boot with a hole in the sole the size of a quarter.

So I went back to the ranch and got Anita and a couple of saddle horses. I told her we were going up to the Luna Flats because Hulsey had a bunch of cattle in there.

We rode the four miles back and chased his cows out of our field. Then we ran them all over to hell and gone, trying to make them break through Hulsey's own fence.

Anita asked me, "Why not just leave the gate open and drive them out?"

I told her, "They're not going out our gate. That's the way they came in. But he'll tell me they broke through the fence on their own, so we'll see to it that they do."

Well, we chased them around till finally they broke through Hulsey's water gap. A water gap is the part of the fence that crosses the stream, made so it gives way in case of a flood and lets the water and whatever it's carrying—brush and logs and debris off the fields—wash past without tearing down too much of the fence.

Then I rode on over to Hulsey's. I found the lazy son where I usually found him, sitting on his porch with his feet up on the banister. I couldn't miss the hole in one of his boot soles. I told him, "I just found your cows in my field."

"Well," he said, "you'll have to strengthen your fences."

I said they never came through the fence, somebody put them in through the gate.

He said, "You don't know anybody put them in through the gate."

I said, "You think a woman can't cut sign? There were tracks all around the gate, horse tracks and boot tracks along with the cow tracks."

He spit a string of tobacco juice over the railing. It splattered on the ground in front of my horse. "I don't know who the hell put them in there. Must have been Ace's kids."

Ace Reynolds was his neighbor.

I just laughed and said, "Well, if they broke through the fence, I just ran them out through your water gap."

Hulsey cussed some more, but he had to rebuild his water gap or he'd've had cows scattered all over the country. All those cows I chased around were heavy and about to calve. That running around never did them any good. But it worked. That ended that. It took some doing to show my neighbors they couldn't run over me. They finally learned, but it took a while. Hulsey started telling around, "You better watch out for that woman. She rides with a 30-30 on her saddle."

Hulsey's neighbor, Ace Reynolds, worked for me every now and then. Once when he stopped at the ranch after checking up on some cows of his that were calving, I said, "Ace, I've got a heifer across Luna Flats about to drop a calf. If you run into her on your way home, I'd appreciate it if you'd head her up here toward the house so I can get her in the corral and take care of her."

I worried about heifers about to calve if they were too far out from the house. Cattle on the range move around and get plenty of exercise and, unlike some cows that are kept in pens, they deliver easy. Still, sometimes they have problems. Now and then I had to deliver a breech-birth calf. I never learned things like that out of a book. I guess it's something you just naturally know how to do, or hear how to do from other people. If the feet come out first you have to push the calf back up in the cow and turn it around so it comes out head-first. Otherwise it might choke on the umbilical before it gets out.

Well, I never heard from Ace and the pregnant heifer never showed up. The kids and I went out looking for her. We hunted for about three days, and we never did find her. When I saw Ace again I asked him, "Did you ever see that heifer down at Luna Flats?"

He said, "No, I never did run into her. She must have gone up one of those canyons and died."

But I'd been up all those canyons and she wasn't there. And if she had died I'd've seen buzzards circling.

Next spring I was coming down from Centerfire, and here were some of Ace's cows lying down on the hillside, resting after they'd drunk at the creek. I rode up there through them, and here was the heifer with my brand showing bright because they had all shed for spring. Beside her was a new calf that had just been freshly branded to Ace.

I chased her up to see if the calf followed her, and it did, so it was hers all right. I went back to the house and got the pickup and drove over to Luna to Ace's house.

"Ace," I told him, "the heifer about to calf that I sent you after last year is up in your pasture with your cows, and she has a young calf with her freshly branded to you. What happened to her calf last year? Was it branded to you, too?"

He said, "I've never seen her up there. I don't know anything about it."

I said, "You'd better find out, because I'm going to report you to the Cattle Grower's Association. I'm a member, and we're going to do something about this."

He said, "Well, I didn't do anything purposely. Dan might have gone up there and branded her."

I said Dan was a nine-year-old kid, he couldn't have gone up there and roped that calf and branded it by himself.

"Well," he said, "what do you want me to do about it?"

I said, "I want you to go up there and get that cow and the calf with her, and bring them to me along with a yearling steer to replace the calf she had last year."

Next day here comes Ace riding up, herding the cow and calf and a yearling steer. We re-branded the calf and the yearling to me, and that was the end of that. It was the last problem I had with those two neighbors. If they pinched any more of my cows I didn't know about it.

But I had fun with a neighbor named Arnold from Pasadena, California, over at the H Bar V. He had a great big ranch that ran from Springerville, Arizona, and joined my upper ranch. In the spring a bunch of his steers mysteriously got into my meadow land and chased my cows around.

I told Arnold a couple of times I didn't want his steers getting in my pasture and chasing my cows because they were all carrying calves. He just laughed and sent some of his cowboys over to move them out, but they always managed with a little help to come back.

So I told him, "If you don't keep them out of here, one of these days I'm going to pick off a nice fat steer and butcher it."

"Aw," he said, "you wouldn't do that."

Sure enough, one day a whole bunch of his steers turned up again in my pasture.

I told Stanley, "Let's get some fresh meat."

I told him to pick out one of those fat steers and run it up the draw there by the lake and kill it, and I'd be down with the pickup and the drag-along—actually a block and tackle.

Stanley did as I told him, and I dragged the steer back to the house. We hung it from a tree and skinned it and threw the offal into the hog pen. The hogs got rid of the evidence in a wink. Then we hung the beef up in the saddle shed. It was a nice beef. I figured from all the grazing it had done on my land, about half the weight on it belonged to me.

The next day or so, here comes Arnold stopping by for a visit. I fed him liver for dinner.

He asked, "Have you been over to Springerville?"

"No," I said, "I haven't."

"Well," he said, "where'd you get this fresh liver?"

I told him, "I just killed one of your steers."

He threw back his head and guffawed. "Aw," he said, "Bob must have come out from Albuquerque."

I let it go at that.

In a week or so, here he comes again. This time I served him roast beef for supper. He asked me again if I had been to Springerville, and I said no, I hadn't been to Springerville.

"Well," he said, "where did you get this fresh meat?"

I said, "I told you, I killed one of your steers."

He laughed his head off at the joke and dived into his dinner.

Anyway, he kept coming over and eating his beef—he didn't like his own cowboys' cooking—but he never did believe me when I said I'd killed one of his beeves. We ate it all up and that was the end of that.

I always turned out my Duroc hogs at Spur Ranch to root out the Jerusalem artichokes I'd planted. Jerusalem Artichokes grow like turnips. They make excellent livestock food. The hogs rooted them up and took a bite, then moved on and rooted up some more. Then I let in the cattle I was fattening for market, and they ate the uprooted artichokes. I had a lot of white-face steers with dirty faces.

One day one of my Duroc hogs strayed quite a ways down, a mile and a half or so, and got into a neighbor's place. I'll never know how the hog got down on the lower end of the ranch. Anyway, this great big Duroc Jersey sow just about ready to have a litter got in the neighbor's popcorn patch. The neighbor drove her out and shot her and left her where she fell.

When I passed by on the road she was very noticeable lying out in the field. I stopped and got out and went to see what was the matter, and found she was dead, she'd been shot. I cut her open and found fifteen dead piglets inside her.

Whenever I saw this neighbor again, I asked, "Did you kill one of my hogs?"

He said, "Yes, I sure as hell did. She come down there and got in my popcorn patch. I'm not going to have any of your animals down here destroying my stuff."

I said, "I'm sorry. I don't know how she got down that far, it's quite a ways." It was a mile or so.

He said, "I'm telling you now and don't forget it, if any more of your stock get down here I'll kill them too."

So I said Okay. But killing stock that strays accidentally is behavior way beyond what's acceptable. Any rancher is going to have stock stray now and then. Well, that wasn't the end of that business.

When the kids left in the fall to attend school in Albuquerque, the loft served as a dorm for Bob's friends who came out to hunt during deer season. I always furnished them with horses and acted as guide. The ranch backed up to a forested area, an animal preserve where hunting wasn't allowed. For the men to hunt I had to lead them farther north, where antelope were plentiful.

A little while after the episode of the murdered hog, I had some Texas deer hunters who always came out in the fall staying at my place. And of course they heard about the episode of the murdered sow. One afternoon they asked me if I would mind going over to Reserve, to Uncle Bill's Bar, to get them a supply of liquor. I thought it was unusual, but I wasn't busy, so I did as they asked.

I was sitting there nursing a drink at Uncle Bill's when a man banged in the door saying something down around Spur Ranch was ablaze. I ran out of there and hurried home. But it wasn't my ranch house. By the time I got there the neighbor's shack was nothing but smoking ashes, the Texans had left for Texas, and I was left with a case of liquor I didn't need.

I have always suspected those Texans sent me to Reserve that day so nobody could blame the fire on me. Texans are known to be unforgiving when it comes to shooting stock. But it was done, and nothing I could do about it.

13 | WINTERS ALONE

After the hunters in the fall, and after the kids were back in school, I was alone on the ranches. I had to ride the trail periodically between the lower and upper ranches, about four miles, to see if the upper ranch headquarters was closed down for the winter. One late fall when we were having little skiffs of snow, and ice forming at night, I was heading up to Centerfire when my horse balked at a narrow pass. The trail going through it was just bare rock, no dirt on it at all. On one side the sheer cliff, and on the other a twenty-five-foot drop.

The horse was afraid to cross it because it looked icy. But I had to get up to Centerfire so I put my spurs to him. That's when I learned the meaning of 'horse sense.' That horse had more sense than I did. Crossing the icy ledge he lost his footing and I could tell he was going down.

I tried to throw off the stirrups and leap free of him, but my toe caught in a stirrup cover. So off we slid into the little canyon. The bottom was nothing but piles of rocks. I landed on my back with the horse on top of me. I'd been raped by the saddle horn.

I managed—I don't know how—to get out from under that half-ton of thrashing animal. I was dazed and bleeding badly, but I could see the horse hadn't broken a leg, he was just trying to get back on his feet.

I dodged his hooves and got him by the front pasterns and turned him over so he could get his footing and stand up. Then, leading him by the reins, I managed somehow to crawl out of that rocky ravine with the horse clambering after me.

At the top I had to sit for a spell on the icy rock to get my breath. I knew something was wrong but I didn't know what. I was losing a lot of blood. I had to do something.

I managed to pull myself back up on my horse. Then I rode several miles back to the house. By the time I got there I was in pretty bad shape. When I slid off the horse I found something had broke. I had a sack of blood hanging down between my legs.

Neither Frank nor Rose was anywhere around. There was nothing for it, whatever had to be done I had to do for myself. I got in the pickup and drove to Springerville. I was in the hospital there for a number of days. An accident like that is the kind of danger you face living out on a ranch by yourself.

But those winters alone on the ranch were some of my happiest times. I liked the solitude. I liked being out there surrounded by wide open spaces. I liked watching wild animals—the deer and coyotes and now and then a mountain lion—and having plenty of time to think without people around. Cows never talk back to you.

For company I had two little screw-tail Boston Bulldogs. They liked to go down to the corral and chase the hogs. One chased a hog while the other grabbed hold of the snout and hung on. Then the hog ran around squealing and trying to shake it loose. When one dog got tired and let go, the other grabbed the snout and they went through the same routine. They kept it up till somebody got down there and broke up their game. It was amazing the way these tough little dogs worked those big hogs.

You hear dogs are near-sighted, but whenever I'd been away from the house and was heading back home, these little bulldogs saw me coming a quarter-mile away and barked their heads off. There was Bootsie, my little Momma dog—she was a real sweetie—and Lulubelle, who didn't like anything or anybody. Little Bootsie would come tearing out hard as she could to meet me. I'd reach down and pick her up and put her in front of me on the saddle, and we'd ride on home together.

She stayed up there on the saddle till I got off and lifted her down. Every once in a while I took her with me if I wasn't going far. She just loved riding horseback.

Wherever there was water, we had a line camp with a trap—a holding pasture—and a little shack to stay in overnight. Most of the line camps were on Centerfire, the upper ranch. I stocked each line shack with a skillet and a coffee pot, and an army cot I hung from the rafters to keep the chipmunks from eating up the canvas.

They're cute little boogers, but they sure can be destructive. I kept the line shacks stocked with canned goods. The chipmunks found glue tasty and ate all the labels off the cans, so you never knew what you'd be having for supper. You just opened the can and found out. I carried my bedroll with me on the saddle when I knew I'd be gone for a day or two. Then I stayed in a line cabin and ate my surprise supper and took the cot down and threw my bedroll on it.

Cattle came in daily for water and the salt lick, and whenever I was riding the fence lines I drove them into the trap to check them for problems like worms. Sometimes after they've been branded the flies get to them as they heal. When that happens you have to catch them and clean them out and disinfect them so they won't get worms. It's one part of ranching that isn't pleasant, but it's something you have to do. You hear talk about the hard work on a ranch. The work is not hard, but if you're going to take care of your livestock you have to pay attention to things and know what you're doing.

In those days there wasn't any robbery or vandalism. We always left the ranch house open, we never locked up anything. Quite often the neighbor cowboys stopped by the house. A couple of them were really nice old guys. One, old Tough Brown, had only one hand. He'd lost the other hand to a buzz saw. Old Tough was one hell of a good cook. He made the best sourdough biscuits you ever tasted.

These old cowboys just came in and made themselves at home. They didn't know if you'd be in that night or off at a line camp, so whatever they saw that needed doing, like feeding the stock and the chickens, why, they took care of it. Many's the time I came home and found Old Tough cooking up venison and sourdough biscuits. It was very pleasant, coming home and finding a nice hot meal cooked up for you.

And if Tough had been there and gone, if he'd got an antelope he always left me a quarter of venison wrapped up in a tarp. Before I built the ice house, I hung meat out at night—it was always cold at night, we were up about nine thousand feet—and took it in before the sun got to it in the morning. Then I put it in a shady place and it stayed cold all day.

With cattle scattered over eleven sections of grazing land—some clear pasture, some timbered—at round-up time, when we cut out the steers to take to market, we had to establish a camp on top of Slaughter Mesa where we could drive them into a makeshift holding corral.

One year, after we'd spent days rounding up the herd, a thunderstorm came up in the night and spooked the cattle. They broke down the corral and scattered all to hell and gone. We had to round them up all over again. After that the kids and I rode the corral fence at night in two-hour shifts, whistling and singing or just talking to the cows to keep them calm.

Once we finished the round-up, we drove them down to Spur Ranch to fatten them up for market. I let them graze there for about a month in the fields I'd planted for that purpose. Then we had a seventy-mile cattle drive across the Plains of St. Augustine to the loading docks on the railroad at Magdalena.

We usually started out with about a hundred and seventy head. The cowboys were my hired man Frank, my daughter Anita, my stepdaughter Dorothy, and two Spanish vaqueros, the Correjos, Grandpa Correjo and a kinsman. We grazed the cattle along the way so they wouldn't lose weight, and we camped at night where there was water for the herd.

It was a very slow business. It took all day to drive the cattle about ten miles. The drive took us about ten days. The first part was through forested land. One cowboy led the herd and the others kept the cattle bunched together and brought the wanderers back in line. I drove the chuck wagon—a truck loaded with all the bedding and food and camp equipment—to the next watering place, and made camp. I had the camp set up and supper cooked by the time the others got in with the herd.

We finally arrived at the Magdalena Driveway, which paralleled the road to Magdalena from Reserve. It was fenced on both sides and between a half mile to a mile wide. Once inside, the cattle couldn't get out. On one drive, the cowpokes made it late to the Driveway and, exhausted, just bedded the cattle and then bedded down themselves without placing a lookout.

The next morning when we woke up the cows were gone. We set out without breakfast looking for them. We found them at the next watering hole. They'd got up in the night and walked all the way there and gone to grazing. Once we found them, cows and cowpokes alike all just settled down for a whole day's rest.

15 I SINGLE AGAIN

About this time I was having little arguments with Bob. I'd learned a lot about ranching, but Bob wasn't a rancher and he didn't understand a lot about running cows. I had arguments with him over things like having to change to a new bull every couple of years. He didn't understand why I couldn't make do with the bull we had.

I kept telling him you need to change bulls ever so often so you won't have incest among your cattle.

He said he didn't give a damn about the cows' morality.

I told him morality had nothing to do with it, incest in the herd leads to inbreeding and weakens your stock.

Anyway, he was always waiting at the end of a cattle drive to pick up the check. On one drive we ran into a snowstorm. It wasn't bad snow, just nasty, spitting snow and sleet, but we were all of us out in the weather. Even our bedding was wet. The miserable conditions made us late getting into Magdalena.

Bob met us fussing that he couldn't waste his time sitting down there waiting for us to get the cattle to Magdalena. He said he needed to get the check and get back to Albuquerque. But of course he couldn't get the check till the cattle was in the Magdalena stockyards.

I told him you can't run cattle on schedule.

He said no and I was as stubborn as a cow and couldn't be run on schedule either.

Well, we had at each other, and of course that got all the help disgruntled. The two Correjos quit and went home and left me there short-handed.

So I told Bob that was it, this was the end of the line. I took off my wedding ring and threw it out there in the St. Augustine Plains. I guess it's still there. We'd been married eight years.

After Bob went back to Albuquerque and a little time passed and the air cleared, he came out to the ranch and stayed overnight to discuss the separation. We had to decide on things he wanted and what I was going to keep.

Before we went to bed I told him, "You'd better get up and get going in the morning while the ground's still frozen. Once it thaws you won't be able to get out." And I offered to fix him an early breakfast.

But he said he would go when he damn well pleased.

He didn't get up till late. Then he enjoyed a breakfast of ham and eggs and my fresh sourdough biscuits, and he loafed around playing with the little dogs till about noon, when he decided to head back to Albuquerque.

He had just bought himself a new car, hadn't had it more than a month or so. He got up the road a way and, sure enough, got stuck in a little ravine the road went through. It had spawned a pretty good mud hole, and his new car sank in with all four wheels.

Disgusted, he walked back to the house and said he'd wait and fool with it in the morning. I said, "You're not going to get it out in the morning. In the morning the car'll be frozen in."

Well, he knew better, so I said Fine.

The next morning he went up there, and of course the wheels were frozen in hard. That car wasn't going anywhere. He hiked back to the house and said, "I guess you better get the tractor and pull me out."

So I fired up the Cat and went up there and watched him hook the chain onto the bumper. I told him that was the wrong way to go about it, that it would never work. In those days cars had leaf springs, and the front bumper was fastened to the body of the car.

But as usual Bob knew better, so I shut up. And when he said "PULL!" I pulled.

I pulled off the whole damn body and left the chassis sitting there frozen in the mud. His new car was a total disaster.

For about two years after Bob and I divorced I was alone all the time on the ranches. Most of the herd was gone, World War II was almost over, and the kids had graduated from high school and set out on their own. Darlene was married and in Albuquerque. Dorothy was going to A&M in Cruces. Anita was working at Kirtland Field as some kind of instructor. I had time on my hands. I never in my life enjoyed being idle, so I was casting around for something to do.

Finally I bought two big semi stock trucks and started hauling cattle and hay for people and bringing in cottonseed cake from Texas. After feeding the stock at dusk, I'd climb on the tractor of one of the semis and maneuver it so the hitch and tongue lined up and connected. Then I rose at three or four next morning, long before first light, and lifted aside the blocks from the wheels and took off under the stars. I'd make it to the next ranch where the hands were waiting to guide the cattle through the chute and into the trailer.

When the cattle was marked for Clovis I needed the early start. Then after delivery it was on to Lubbock for stock feed or well casing for a neighbor's well. I was often away from the ranch three days at a time. Nights on the road I might have whiskey and gossip in a local bar with other truckers. We talked about the war in Europe like we knew what it was all about, but nobody really knew. One thing I was sure of from World War I—whatever we got out of it, it wouldn't be worth all the killing. But nothing I could do about it, so I let it go.

Before I took off on a trip one morning, I stole a few eggs from under a setting hen and slipped some duck eggs in their place. The hen just readjusted the eggs under her and settled back down.

Three days later when I got back to the ranch, tired and hungry, I went first to check on the hen and found her clucking over six fluffy balls of yellow fuzz. She'd hatched the ducklings. I let mother and chicks out of the shed to explore the place, then unloaded the trailer and went to the house to get some shuteye.

Later, wakened by a commotion in the lower pasture, I got up and went to investigate. Well, the ducklings had found their natural element. The little things were paddling around in the middle of the pond, while the mother hen was running and squawking back and forth at the edge of the pond, flapping her wings like she was trying to fly to save her babies from a watery death. But the ducklings ignored her, circling happily in the water some distance from shore.

I was awake by then, so I went on about my business. I saddled up and rode into the leased forest land up above the main house to check on the scrap of a herd I still maintained. I didn't get back till twilight, and there were the ducklings, all asleep, piled up together for warmth in a hummock of grass.

It looked like the wind had blown an old feed sack out in the pond, so I got the net and dragged it to shore. What I fished in was a soggy body. The poor mother hen had braved the water to try and rescue her chicks, but chickens have never been known to swim.

Her death was my fault for interfering with nature. I should have known better. There the poor thing lay, a testament to my foolishness. But too late to think of that, I'd already done it.

The coyotes were yipping not far away. They'd soon be prowling, scavenging the fields and arroyos. So I gathered up the ducklings and put them in the shed where they'd be safe. After I cleaned and plucked the hen and put her in the ice house—no need to let good meat go to waste—I drew my pot of beans out of the well where I'd dropped it on a rope to keep it cool, and went on in the house and had my supper.

I had a number of adventures trucking. One time I went over to Morenci, the valley across the mountain from Mule Creek Pass, to get a load of hay. Coming up over the pass on the way back I had to go through a tunnel. I didn't realize my load was too high, and coming through the tunnel I raked the whole top layer of hay off my semi.

I didn't have anybody with me, I was by myself. It was about two A.M. Nothing to do but park the truck on the far side and drag the hay bales through the tunnel and out to the truck. Then I had to stack the hay up in stair steps to lift it back on the truck, and then stack it on the truck. That was the last time I brought hay over from that side of the mountain. After that I always got it from Cruces.

Another time, the Forest Service had gathered up a bunch of wild horses and horses that people had turned loose. They were selling them for two dollars a head. So I went over to Springerville and gathered up twenty of these horses and loaded them on the semi stock truck to take over to Phoenix and sell them.

But to get to Phoenix I had to go down the steep grade of Salt River Canyon. I discovered the hard way that my load was too heavy on that steep, twisting canyon road. I'd no sooner started down when I heard a loud pop. I knew what had happened. I'd blown out the hoses on my air brakes.

The road was full of curves with the canyon wall on one side and the steep drop on the other. The only thing I could do to slow the truck was shave the embankment on the high side of the road.

Well, I bounced off that canyon wall all the way down. You never heard such a racket. It was just luck I didn't meet any cars as I careened around those bends. Somehow I managed to more or less hold the road and not go off into the canyon with that bunch of horses.

When I finally made it to the bottom and coasted to a stop, I pulled myself together and got out. The whole side of the truck was smashed in from shaving the bank. I opened the tailgate and checked on the horses. They were shook up too, but they were all right. So I reconnected the air hoses and climbed in and headed on in to Phoenix.

I had two trucks, and the trucking business kept me busy. When the weather was bad, I had to go in and out of the ranch road on a freeze, waiting till it was frozen at night before heading out and coming in before ten in the morning when it thawed.

One time I had a load of cattle to take from Luna to the railhead at Silver City. To get to Silver from Luna Valley you had go up the steep grade of South Mountain. They had cleaned the snow off the road with a grader, and I got off with the cattle about ten that night.

About halfway up South Mountain I hit a sheet of black ice. My tires lost traction and I started skidding. I managed to get the rig stopped, but whenever I pulled up a ways and got a little footing, the trailer slid closer to the canyon. Well, I thought, here goes the trailer with a whole load of cattle into the draw.

After I managed to stop, I got out and slid under the trailer with my hatchet and chopped ice between the wheels till morning.

I finally got over South Mountain and late into Silver City with the cattle. They had been holding the train for this bunch of cows. When I pulled into the stockyards, the irate cattle buyer came over yelling, "Leave it to a woman! If you don't want a thing done right, just leave it to a woman!"

After the night I'd been through, that made me pretty disgusted. I threw the keys down on the ground and left him there and went over to the Murray Hotel.

One old cattle buyer looked up from his newspaper in the lobby and said, "Frances, where'd you get those green Levis?"

I was covered with cow shit from head to foot from digging out snow and ice all night underneath that trailerload of cows. They'd let go on me whenever the spirit moved them.

Over in the stockyard, the cattle buyer couldn't find anybody would touch my truck. It wasn't their truck and they weren't going to have anything to do with it. He had to come up to the hotel and apologize.

Then I went back down and backed the truck up to the chute so they could unload the cattle and get them on the train.

That year Anita and I had planned to meet in El Paso and spend Christmas together there and in Juarez, where we could visit our friend Rosachita.

I got there early and booked a room at the Paseo Del Norte Hotel. I waited and waited, then waited some more, but Anita didn't show up. Christmas came and went and still I hadn't heard from her. I finally got hold of one of her girl friends in Albuquerque and found out she had taken off for some place in Utah to marry one of the fliers from the Air Force base.

It was one of the biggest disappointments of my life. I didn't meet this son-in-law until they'd been married for several years. Anita didn't come home, never wrote me. There was no way I could get in touch with her. I didn't know where she was. I'd had another husband picked out for her that I guess didn't suit. I should have known better, it was my mother picked out Parker for me.

Anita was a beautiful, charming girl.

After the herd was sold, the only ranch stock was a few cows and chickens and the little dogs. Without the kids and the cows to keep me busy, I was alone on the ranch most of the time. When that had gone on long enough, I decided to sell out. First we sold out the upper ranch, Centerfire. Bob got the money out of that. Then some Mormon neighbors bought Spur Ranch.

But I'd done pretty well with ranching. Mortgages at that time weren't like they are today. Today it's two hundred, three hundred thousand dollars. At that time it was twenty thousand, twenty-five thousand, maybe up as high as thirty thousand. It was a big indebtedness then, but thinking about it now, it doesn't sound like very much really.

I was thirty-six years old when I went out to Catron County, and I was fifty when we sold out. That's fourteen years I spent on the ranches. I was probably a success at ranching because I loved what I was doing, all of it, the long winters, the work, the troublesome neighbors. We managed to buy the ranches. After the first five years, both the ranches were paid for. With the kids gone, the ranches gone, the marriage with Bob over, and trucking a lonesome way of life, I was rattling around like a nut in an empty can. I had to cast around and think what I wanted to do next.

17 ▮ I BUILD A ROADHOUSE

After selling the ranches, I bought a couple hundred acres, approximately a township, at the location of the old Navajo Lodge in Datil. The original lodge had been a ranch house up in the mountains in White House Canyon, nine miles out of Datil. About forty years before I bought the place, Ray Morley, who owned the ranch, had taken the old house apart and moved it log by log down to Highway 60, a much-traveled route then, where he put it back together and renamed it The Navajo Lodge. It was built of rough-hewn, square-cut logs. Two stories high with gabled ends and a big center hall with a tall stone fireplace climbing up the front, it was very picturesque.

Ray Morley was the brother of Agnes Morley Cleveland, who wrote NO LIFE FOR A LADY. Coming out here from the East and messing around with ranches and cattle, I felt like part of that book. Their mother practically started the town of Datil single-handed. She was the post-mistress, and she it was who talked her son Ray into moving the old ranch house down to the highway. Datil was built on the sight of Camp Datil, established in the 1800s by General Miles to protect people from the roving bands of Apaches under Geronimo.

Ray Morley added several Navajo families to the place to give it local color. Travelers got to watch the Navajo women weaving their blankets, which they could also buy if they liked. Morley learned rattlesnake handling from the Indians, which he liked to demonstrate to gawping tourists.

After Morley died, for a time the lodge continued as a hotel, but in the early forties it had burned to the ground. I thought I'd get in there and run one of these roadside joints, but first I had to clean away the debris of the old burned-down wreck. Once that was done, I started to rebuild.

I didn't have enough finances to build the big institution I had in mind. I had to start from scratch and put in the foundations myself, mixing the cement and all. You had a hard time buying any kind of supplies right after the war. This was around in about '48. And getting plumbing supplies in particular was pretty near impossible. I was picking up supplies out of Army-Navy stores and different places in El Paso and Las Cruces, anywhere I could find them. But I did what I'd set out to do. Getting help where I could, and doing a lot of the work myself, I rebuilt the old Navajo Lodge.

The lobby of my lodge, with the bar at one end, was about twenty-five by fifty feet. It had a huge big fireplace with everybody's brand from the ranches around there embedded in the stones. Later I added eight or ten slab cabins. I did the plumbing in all those cabins myself—threading pipes, burying them in the ground, and connecting them. I put in those bathrooms myself, as well as the bathrooms in the main lodge building, which had eleven hotel rooms.

I was finishing up the last of the lodge when I realized I had to build a separate cafe. I'd been trying to serve light eats in the bar and there just wasn't enough room. So I went ahead and started the cafe addition onto the main building.

Getting supplies together I had overdrawn at the bank somewhere in the neighborhood of five thousand dollars. Hard as I tried, I couldn't think how I was going to finish what I had started. Mr. Becker at the bank in Belen had written me several times about my overdrafts.

I wrote back and told him I didn't know how I would catch up but I would catch up somehow.

One day when I was dumping cement in the wheelbarrow and running the floor in the cafe building, Mr. Becker came by on his way home to Albuquerque. He'd been down to Reserve. I had a cement mixer going, one of those small ones, and I was about ready for the last load of the day.

He asked me, "How much money do you think it'd take for you to finish up this project?"

"Mr. Becker," I said, "I don't have any idea."

"Well," he said, "you certainly work at it hard enough."

I told him, "If you want to talk to me you'll have to wait till I get this load of cement out of this wheelbarrow or it'll harden before I can do anything with it."

So he sat down on a stack of concrete blocks, and I went on and emptied my wheelbarrow. Then I washed up the mixer and went over and sat with him.

"Well," he said, "give me an idea of what you're planning to do. What's the rest of the work to be done around here?" He said, "I want you to write me up a list of what you have to do to finish it."

So I made a list of what I thought had to be done, but I didn't have any idea what the cost was going to be.

"Well," he said, putting the list in his pocket, "we'll see what we can do, but we can't go on with this overdraft business."

I said I realized that. I said I might just have to sell the place as is.

He told me he'd be back in touch with me in a few days. And pretty soon I get a letter from him saying, "Please stop in at the Belen bank the first time it's convenient." Signed, "L. C. Becker."

So I thought, Well this is it, the bank's going to take over what I've done on the place, and I can't do anything about it. My plans had been to have the bar and the cafe going, and rent out all these cabins and rooms. I figured the place would pay itself off pretty well that way. But I didn't have it all done yet, not by a long shot.

So I drove in to the bank in Belen prepared to face the music.

When I got ushered into his office, I knew I was about to lose the lodge. But instead of foreclosing on me L. C. Becker said, "We've decided to lend you thirty-five thousand dollars to finish your project out there, which of course will also take care of your overdraft."

Well, I was stunned. "Mr. Becker," I said, "I never had thirty-five thousand dollars, I never expect to have thirty-five thousand dollars, and you're doing this at your own risk."

But he went ahead and loaned me the money, and I finished the place off—the lodge and the cafe and the cabins. Pretty soon I was filling the lodge every night, selling drinks in the bar and dinners in the cafe, and regularly renting out the cabins and the lodge rooms. I had a going business. The place was making money.

The cafe I built had a horseshoe counter, hand-made and beautiful, all polished wood three or four inches thick, with the kitchen in back. As chief cook and bottle washer, I was in there five o'clock in the morning, cooking, and I stayed there till twelve noon, when the other cook came on. After a morning in the cafe I rested for an hour or two, then came back and tended bar in the lodge from two in the afternoon till two at night. On weekends I baked as many as forty pies at a time, and I made great big preserving pots full of chili. The boys from the School of Mines in Socorro came up every weekend, and they took a lot of chili back to school with them. Once I had the bar going, I had to go down to El Paso every now and then because that was still the only place you could buy good liquor. Pretty soon I had more work than I could tend to.

I was a good ranch cook. I could cook sourdough biscuits and beans, and my chili was the best in the county, and I could turn venison into a gourmet delicacy. But living in New Mexico there were some dishes I was ignorant about. So when I ordered some shrimp out of El Paso, I just breaded them like they came and cooked them and served them up.

All of a sudden I heard a big commotion out in the restaurant. The waitress brought back one of the plates. That's when I saw the shells.

It was a good thing a professional cook named Gene, a little crippled man, came along about then, wanting a job cooking at the lodge. He had been a cook at Lake Tahoe in the wintertime. I thought I could learn a lot about cooking from him. And sure enough Gene was a big help.

It seemed like people just showed up whenever I needed them. After Gene, along came a dealer from the casinos in Las Vegas, Nevada, wanting to work for me. He was a man in his sixties with a young wife, Rachel, in her twenties, who'd been a dealer too.

The dealer and his wife ran in a few poker games at night, and that helped out with the overhead. I also got some slot machines, but they didn't last, they got picked up. But they didn't catch the poker games.

We had a lot of fun working in the cafe. Rachel, the gambler's wife, began to tend bar for me. She won more money with the dice cup than she made selling drinks. Rachel was full of jokes. When she got hungry she'd yell out, "Bring me some french fried rabbit tracks!" And the waitress would take her meal to her in the bar.

Down in the pasture one day I saw some rabbit tracks hardened in the mud. I cut them out and brought them back to the Lodge and battered them and deep fried them till they looked real pretty. The next time Rachel ordered french fried rabbit tracks, I sent her some.

One day old man Ringer—he had a big ranch up in Catron County—told me to get one dozen steaks together because he was going to bring over a party of people that night for dinner. So I took the steaks out of the deep freeze and thawed them, and when his party came in that night I got busy cooking them up.

I had the whole stove top full of steaks when I stepped back onto something soft. Oh my gosh, I thought I'd dropped one of the steaks and I didn't have any extras thawed, and all those folks waiting for their dinner.

Then old Winnie, who helped me in the kitchen, spoke up. "Frances, let me know when you plan to get off my foot."

She'd bided her time and let me sweat.

For some reason, in the fall of the year the deer always came down to the highway every night. One night while her husband got the game warden in a poker game, Rachel and I went out in the pickup to poach us some venison with a spotlight.

We came upon about five bucks on the highway, and Rachel picked one out and shot him. The buck fell down in the bar ditch.

I told her to get out and hide down in the ditch with the deer and throw some rabbit brush on the road to mark where she was. Then I drove off a way and made sure nobody was coming before I turned around and went back to load up Rachel and the deer.

Well, we didn't need the rabbit brush. Rachel was down in the ditch bending over the deer, sure she was hiding from whoever drove by. But as I came along I saw her behind sticking up like a hot air balloon. You couldn't miss Rachel. She was right hefty.

Anyway, I picked up her and the buck, and we got it home and hidden before the game warden finished his poker game.

Another night I was coming home from buying supplies in Socorro with a fellow named Jim, who used to come out from Texas to do some hunting. We came upon a buck, and Jim wanted to take it back to Texas with him. So he shot it and tossed it in the trunk of my car, and I took off in a hurry.

We weren't hardly any way down the road when that buck came alive and raised a racket like you never heard. I jammed on the breaks, Jim opened the trunk, the deer jumped out, and Jim killed it all over again.

But that buck had played havoc with the trunk of my brand new Buick car. I wondered how I could ever explain how those dents pocked out instead of in. To get the body work done I took the car well away from home, all the way to Flagstaff, so my poaching wouldn't be exposed.

The guy at the Flagstaff body shop said, "I've seen cars with dints all over them, but never from the inside out."

I had my story ready. I told him I was carrying some rock in the trunk, and when I was bumping over a real rough road the rocks bounced up and dinted the trunk lid.

I don't think he believed me. But that was my story and I stuck to it.

In time, to get some R & R away from the lodge, I bought a nice little spread, the Crosby Springs Ranch, in the mountains out of Datil. Pretty soon pet deer started coming up to the corral to drink, so I took cake up there for them. It got to where when they heard my car they came out and waited for me—momma deer with their babies. But if I went up in somebody else's car you wouldn't see hide nor hair of them.

Along with these deer, I had a number of pets while I was in Datil. A traveling salesman gave me a little monkey that became quite an entertainment at the lodge. The monkey liked beer, and the customers would give him a drink now and then. And of course all the drunks teased the monkey and that got him mad.

Some time before, I'd shot a mountain lion that had killed a fawn out on my place, and I had the lion mounted over the fireplace in the lobby. That little monkey took out all his frustrations on the mountain lion. He'd climb up there and get on the lion and squeeze him and beat the living hell out of him. The monkey finally got to be too much, so I gave him to the zoo in Albuquerque.

And once when I was hauling cattle for a rodeo over in Pie Town under the Sawtooth Range—I'd kept one of my big trucks—I was waiting for the rodeo to be over so I could take the cattle back home when along comes an Airdale dog and lays down under my truck. She seemed deathly tired. I coaxed her out and sweet-talked her, and she wanted to get in the truck. When I examined her I found her pads were all worn. She must have come a long distance. So I took her home with me.

One day a fellow from over by the Malpais near Grants stopped by the lodge and recognized her. He had bought her from some people and taken her home with him, but she'd run away and I guess was heading back to where she came from when she stopped to rest under my cattle truck.

Well, she was his and the fellow still wanted her, so he took her back to Grants. But this was a traveling dog. In about ten days she showed up back at the lodge. This time he let me keep her. She was a wonderful watchdog. I named her Susie. I had her a number of years.

Meanwhile I'd been made deputy sheriff in Catron County, and now and then I had to exercise that office.

Old man Redding, from over in Amarillo, had caught his wife with another guy and shot her. When he got acquitted for the killing, he moved to Catron County and bought a ranch down in Horse Springs, between Reserve and Datil. He got to be one of the regulars at the lodge.

Pretty soon he remarried a red-headed waitress named Frieda from over in Socorro. Maybe she hadn't heard of his marital reputation. He was a mean old buzzard. First thing you know, he starts beating up on Frieda. She came in a couple of times and complained to me about what was going on. I didn't relish a dead wife on my watch. I warned him if he didn't stop I'd have to come out there to the ranch and arrest him.

"You come on out," he said. "It'll take you and the Texas Rangers to haul me in."

Sure enough, one day a fellow ran in the lodge and told me old man Redding was parked outside beating up on Frieda. She had her suitcase with her, about to leave him, and he didn't take to the idea.

He'd come after her and yanked open her car door and thrown the suitcase out in the parking lot. Her bras and panties were blowing all over the desert in the wind, decorating the limbs of the cactus and hanging up on the sage. So Frieda got hold of his face and grabbed out his false teeth and threw them out in the parking lot, and along came somebody in a pickup and pulled in and ran over them.

Well, I got husband and wife separated. He was walking around out there picking up his false teeth in pieces, and we gathered up what bits of Frieda's laundry we could find. Then I took old man Redding to the lock-up in Socorro.

I had similar trouble with this fellow Utah Ike, a rodeo cowboy. Ike was a mean bastard. He would bet money he could break a Coke bottle over his head, and he'd do it. Maybe that's why he didn't have much sense.

A woman named Mabel from Brownwood, Texas, who was married to a doctor, fell for Ike and left this doctor husband for him. Ike was about twenty-five. He'd already been married once and had two kids. Mabel was older than Ike, maybe about forty-five, but a good-looking woman. She was going to straighten Utah out. Mabel had money—I don't know where she got it—and she spent it on Ike as if it flowed like water. She bought them a little farm out at Pie town.

Every time Utah got drunk he got mean. If there wasn't a guy around to pick on, he'd pick on Mabel. One Saturday night when they came in the bar and started drinking, I warned him. "Utah," I said, "I don't want you starting any trouble tonight. You do and I'm taking you down to Socorro."

He said he'd behave himself. But along about midnight he started getting rough, so I put him out. I told him to go home and behave himself.

Next morning here he comes, looking for Mabel. I asked him where she was, why she wasn't at home, and if he'd been beating on her. He said he hadn't laid a hand on her and he begged me to go find her.

So I took Margaret, one of the waitresses, with me and went looking for Mabel. We stopped and asked questions at every farm house on the way out to their place. When we finally found her at a neighbor's I wouldn't have recognized her she was beaten so bad.

I told her, "Mabel, this has gone far enough. I have to go get him." She said she was through with him. She swore out a warrant, and I went after Ike. I found him out at their little ranch with his two young kids.

When I drove up to the front gate, they all three came out in the yard, Utah with his arm hanging at his side, weighted down by the pistol in his hand.

I said, "Ike, I don't have to tell you what you did to Mabel last night."

He said, "I guess I did get a little out of line, but I only hit her a few times."

I told him I'd come to take him to Socorro.

He called me a few unseemly names and said, "I ain't going anywhere with you and don't you come any closer." He raised the pistol and pointed it at me.

I handed Margaret my 38 and told her, "If he tries anything, just shoot the son of a bitch." And I started toward him.

About then his ten-year-old spoke up. "Daddy, did you forget that gun ain't loaded?"

Well, Ike swatted the kid and lowered his gun and toed the dirt a minute. Then he asked me where Mabel was.

"She's on her way to the hospital in Socorro," I told him, "and you're on your way to the Socorro jail."

I put the roughneck in the front seat and got in the back holding the gun on him while Margaret drove. If there was any shooting to be done, I'd be the one to do it.

In Socorro we went before the judge. The judge told Utah to get out of New Mexico and if he ever came back it would go hard on him.

Once the lodge was well on its feet, I was able to take off three winters straight and go down to Mexico for a couple weeks of fishing.

One winter I went fishing in Encinata with Bill and Maggie Guiness. They'd worked for me in Catron County and we'd got to be friends. Maggie loved to fish. They were both good sports. Bill was a one-legged guy with a drinking problem, maybe because he was always in a lot of pain. He was sleeping one off back at the motel one day and Maggie and I were out fishing off the pier when in comes a fellow with his lobster traps. We bought four or five lobsters and took them back to the motel and put them in the shower and turned it on low, then went back to fishing.

When Bill woke up he made it to the shower hopping without his crutch. We heard him yelling all the way down to the pier. He'd opened the shower door and seen all the lobsters crawling around in there. Thinking he had the D.T.s, he'd fallen down on the floor and was writhing around, screaming his head off. That experience led him to give up drinking spirits.

Another time I went to Guaymas with the Doaks, a couple who had a tourist court in Albuquerque. We rented a fishing boat and went out for the day in the Sea of Cortez. It turned out to be a long day. There were sharks and killer whales swimming around out there, but they weren't bothering us and we were catching a lot of fish. But then a shark as big as the boat took the mullet on one of our lines. Now this looked to be a different story.

He made a big run for it and spun the reel till we were almost out of line. The skipper yelled, "Tie on another line!" When the shark swam up to the boat again, the skipper was all set to spear it.

But I thought that would be a mistake—a shark that size hooked to the end of our line could upset the boat. So I yanked out a knife and cut the line. The skipper made a few choice remarks, but that was the last we saw of the shark.

During the scare, the boat's motor had conked out. The skipper thought it was the battery. We saw other boats, but he wouldn't hail them, he was sure he could get the motor started. He kept trying, but without any luck. Turned out it was the distributor cap. No way he was going to start that motor.

We were in one hell of a fix. Here we were, sloshing around in the middle of the Sea of Cortez. The sun went down and the wind came up. One minute we were up on a mountain of waves and the next we'd slide down a watery gully.

Twilight came, and then dark. After a while we began to see planes out looking for us, but without lights and in that dark spread of water, there was no chance they'd see us. That went on for some time, till finally they sent out a sub-chaser. It found us and towed us back in.

In spite of our trouble, we had a big catch, a hundred and fifty pounds of fish. When we asked the skipper next day what he'd done with our fish, he said the fish had spoiled. But we couldn't help noticing all the restaurants were advertising fresh fish that day. I guess the skipper saw to it he could afford to get his motor fixed.

The lodge in Datil was bringing in money when here comes my daughter Anita and my son-in-law Buzz. After staying with me a little while, they decided they wanted to take over the lodge and run it. My son-in-law had been a lieutenant colonel in the Air Force, but he got out before he could take his retirement, so he needed something to do.

By that time I was tired of working so hard, so I let them have the business. I bought a small ranch in Mountainair and went over there to live. It had a beautiful great big house. But the well pump was wind-generated. I spent half my time sitting on top of the windmill, fitting the cogs back in so I could get water to the fifty head of Black Angus I was running. After about a year, Buzz and Anita had run the lodge in the red. I had to go back to Datil and take over the place again, and they moved into my place in Mountainair.

By then I was tired of dealing with the public on a daily basis. And there'd been some talk about changing the road. If they did that, the lodge would no longer be on the main highway. So I started thinking I'd better do something with this outfit.

One day some people from Iowa came in and were giving me a lot of static. I made an egg sandwich about five or six different ways with the same egg for an old lady who first wanted it poached, then wanted it scrambled, then didn't want it at all. After these Iowa people informed me how bad the place was run, I put a sign up over the kitchen window: IF YOU DON'T LIKE THE WAY THIS PLACE IS RUN GIVE THE OWNER NINETY-FIVE THOUSAND DOLLARS AND RUN IT TO SUIT YOURSELF.

I no sooner got the sign up when along comes this prune picker from California and asks Rachel, "Where's your boss?"

She told him, "She's in the kitchen."

He said, "I'd like to talk to her."

I went out there thinking he was going to complain about his eggs or tell me I'd burnt his toast. Instead he said, "Does that sign up there mean what it says?"

I told him, "It certainly does."

"Well," he said, "I'm going on vacation to Oklahoma. When I come back through here in about two weeks I'd like to talk to you about a trade."

I said fine, never expecting to see him again, but in about two weeks here he comes.

"I ain't got no money," he said, "but I've got two houses in Grandina, California. I'll trade you my equity in those houses as down payment on this place."

So I said, "Okay."

He said he still owed around nine thousand dollars on the houses out in California, and he asked me when I'd come out and look at them. I told him I didn't need to come out and look at them, I'd get an appraiser out there, a good real estate person, to look at them for me.

I got those houses dirt cheap because the termites feasting on them were about down to the bone. The deal settled with him still owing me in the neighborhood of seventy-five thousand dollars on the lodge.

By then the balance I owed the bank was low. I sold the houses in California and paid it off. I had cash left over, and on top of that I had the income from the mortgage I was holding on the lodge to invest someplace else. That was all well and good, but once again I was out of a job and looking for something to do.

19 | TURKEY FARMING

First, I built a big house out on the Datil ranch. I planned to raise chickens and turkeys out there. Rachel's husband had been very sick. He'd been in the hospital in Socorro. After he died, Rachel was at loose ends, so she came in with me on the chicken and turkey business. Once we got this brood business going, we had several hundred turkeys and quite a few chickens.

To heat the brooder houses we buried barrels in the ground and ran electric heat through them. The turkeys were getting up to a pretty good size when one morning I woke up to find the whole thing going up in flames. The brooder houses had caught fire from the wiring. I ran out there and threw out all the turkeys I could, and neighbors rushed over and helped. We saved most of the birds.

They were contracted to a market in Albuquerque, so we put them in an old barn that was on the place till Thanksgiving time rolled around. Then we had to kill and pluck and draw every one of them. For a couple of weeks I had all the women from miles around picking pin feathers out of turkeys.

I had to come up with some way to freeze them. It was November and getting pretty cold, so we filled the stock tank and tossed them in and froze them in the water. Then when it came time, we chipped them out and loaded them in the truck and Rachel took them to Albuquerque and sold them.

After the turkey adventure she decided to return to Texarkana because her parents were getting up in years. Rachel had been my gambler and my deer-poaching partner, but back in Texas she got religion through Oral Roberts. She was writing me letters every other day, trying to convert me. But I never put much stock in the churches. My religion was between me and the Man Upstairs. She gave up in about six months, but we've always kept in touch.

I was alone out there on the turkey ranch when one night after I'd gone to bed a black widow spider fell from a viga and got under the covers and bit me on the leg. It was too late at night to go to the hospital. So I went in my office and wrote a note that said, "If you find me dead, this black widow spider was the killer." I pinned the spider to the note so people would know what had happened to me.

But I woke up alive next morning. My leg swelled up and got a little numb. It was sore for a while. The spider hadn't solved any problem for me, I was still at loose ends.

One day when I stopped by the bank in Belen, Mrs. Herlihy, who worked there, said, "Frances, why don't you quit working so hard and do some investing with us?"

I told her I didn't have enough money to invest in anything.

She said, "Oh yes you do. In these times a lot of people come near losing their property. If you pay them for their equity, instead of getting foreclosed they get their money out of it. Once you own the property we can carry your balance here at the bank just as we carried it on the lodge. In other words, you just assume the loan. Then you can rent the place or sell it, do whatever suits you. And you're in the real estate business."

Not having anything better to do, I followed her suggestion. I got my license and built an office onto the ranch house in Datil and went into real estate.

By now I was a grandma. Anita and Buzz had several children, three girls and a boy. They'd been living on the ranch in Mountainair, but Buzz decided he wasn't cut out for a rancher. He wanted to go into business hauling limestone for a cement plant outside of Albuquerque in Tijeras Canyon. For that he needed heavy equipment.

So I put my Black Angus on rented pasture in Mora and traded the place at Mountainair and went on a note with him to buy two hydraulic trucks and a bulldozer. He moved the family into Albuquerque.

Ever since I was a little kid on the wheat farm in Kansas, I'd kept up with my stepsister Doris Bichel. She'd been teaching all these years in Michigan, but now she decided to come out west and teach on the Zuni reservation. She spent the summer with me on the little ranch I still had in Datil, and for a spell we got into the dog business, with kennels in Albuquerque and Socorro. Doris ran the one in Albuquerque and a nurse friend of hers from the reservation ran the one in Socorro. I helped with the financial end of things, but otherwise I wasn't much involved.

I was doing a little real estate business, but it looked like I couldn't get ranching out of my blood. That spring I traded the turkey ranch in Datil for a larger spread at Eagle Nest and moved my cattle up from Mora. The Eagle Nest ranch was a beautiful place. A hill on the ranch later became the site of the Vietnam Memorial the fellow built to honor his son who died over there.

I got Maggie and Bill Guiness, my fishing buddies, to come take care of the cattle. And Doris came up during school vacation. I was spending the summer fishing the Cimarron River without a notion in my head of what a winter in Eagle Nest was like.

Fall went by and winter set in. Then it started to snow. When the snow got up past the windowsills and I had to hire somebody with a bulldozer to come clear the road so I could get to Cimarron for stock feed, I decided the place was too cold for my mother cows and too cold for me. I loaded the cattle in stock trucks and moved them back to Mora for the rest of the winter.

During the thaw I sold that ranch. Then in the spring I moved to Taos.

21 I IN TAOS WITH DOUGHBELLY PRICE

I'd met Doughbelly Price while I was still working Spur Ranch and Centerfire. His brother, an old cattle buyer, had a store in Apache Creek. I met Doughbelly while he was visiting this brother, and Doughbelly had come out to the ranches. He was an entertaining fellow. Earlier in his life he'd been a gambler, a bootlegger, and a bronc rider. As gambler he'd been a shill, and he was famous in his day as a bronc rider. He won the southwest championship at the big rodeo in Las Vegas, NM in 1925. Doughbelly could poke fun at himself. He liked to tell about the time in his bronc riding career when he beat the horse out of the chute.

When I met him, he was writing political satire for the Taos newspaper in the style of Will Rogers, only rougher. But he was also in the real estate business. I had to find something to do, and all I knew to do with myself then was to get into real estate in earnest. So once in Taos I went to see him.

I learned that Doughbelly and I had a few things in common. He said he'd made enough bootleg whiskey to float a battleship, and he'd once been a blues singer. But I did my blues singing in nightclubs and he did his in a minstrel show.

He had also been in the movies. He was a chariot driver in the first Ben Hur picture. And when he departed what he always called the city of Lost Angels, like me he'd headed for New Mexico in a Model T Ford. He told people it had no top, no windshield, and very little Ford. Like me he had trouble going over a pass—this one near San Bernardino. He said in that open car he like to froze to death. The Ford never made it back to New Mexico, but Doughbelly did.

He'd often been called Little Man because he wasn't more than five-foot-four-inches tall. He said he'd never met a pair of stirrups he didn't have to shorten. But he was all man. He claimed that all his life he'd liked wild horses, wild steers, and wild women.

He wasn't called Doughbelly because he had a big belly. He got the name one time when he was just a kid and already working as a cowboy. He was a cowboy by the time he was fifteen. The job of cowboy and camp cook often went together, so he'd also been camp cook. He told about one drive over in Arizona when he'd packed his kitchen on four burros as there were no such things as wagons as there were no such things as roads. Anyway, while he was camp cook, one day he turned over a big pan of sourdough biscuit mash all over himself. Even his boots were full of it. He was scraping off all he could with a kitchen knife when somebody came by and saw him and yelled, "Well, if you're not a doughbelly!" The name stuck. He was Doughbelly the rest of his life.

Anyway, I dropped in to see him once I got to Taos and asked him if he knew of an office I could rent, or if he had one vacant.

He said, "Sure, you can move in here with me and we can both starve together."

His location was right on the corner of Bent Street, across from the Taos Inn. He called his office "the clip joint." Setting up my office with him gave me a chance to be entertained while getting acquainted with Taos people and finding out if I could do any good in real estate.

One of the first things Doughbelly told me was, "You can't do business in Taos with the Spanish people because they all hate gringos."

So I made it a point to make Spanish friends. I got to know the

Martinez and Torres families, sheep people in Taos, and I made a few pretty good deals.

I rented desk space in Doughbelly's office for about two years, till it got to where Doughbelly wanted part of my commissions. But I wasn't his salesman, I was an independent broker myself. So when he moved Charley Brooks's collection agency into the place I decided that wouldn't be good for business. It was time for me to move on, but Doughbelly and I and his wife stayed friends for years to come.

After that I had my business—The Northern New Mexico Real Estate Exchange—just off the plaza, next to the First State Bank, which occupied the corner site of the old Columbian Hotel, and later I moved in back of that to an office on Placitas.

My office was like an old-timey general store, a place with a big wood stove where people dropped in and put up their feet and visited. I usually had a couple of sales people in there working for me. As the office was an old store front, I put cactus and bleached animal skulls and old saddles and spurs in the windows to give people something to look at.

I wasn't sure I could make it just selling real estate, so I started buying old fixer-upper houses when they came on the market. All day I was either at the office or out showing land and houses and getting to know Taos County, but in the evenings I was painting and plumbing and putting down tile and in general renovating some old place till it was fit to sell.

Whenever I bought a place I lived in it while I fixed it up. Then I sold it and did the same deal over again. That way I lived in quite a number of places in Taos—Colonias, Talpa, Lower Ranchitos, Ranchos, once in a while in town. I got to know every Taos neighborhood real well.

Back when my son-in-law decided he wasn't into ranching and moved Anita and the kids to Albuquerque, I'd traded the little ranch in Mountainair for a piece of land down in Martin, Texas. The Texas land was all mesquite, but it had water rights and it adjoined irrigated cotton land. That made it more or less valuable.

A guy in Taos wanted to swap me some sage land he owned for the Texas land. His sage land—129 acres in Lower Colonias—was valued at only five or ten dollars an acre, but I traded with him because I had no use for land in Texas. He knew the Texas land and thought somebody would buy it from him because it had water rights.

In the 1950s nobody around Taos figured sagebrush land was worth anything. Doughbelly said, "What in hell're you going to do with sagebrush land?" He said it would take a barrel of water and a bale of hay to get a jackrabbit across that country.

"Well," I said, "I don't know. If I've got some of it maybe somebody else will want a little."

"Ay God," he said, "out there it'll be five hundred degrees in the shade, and there ain't no shade. And where in hell will they get any water?"

"Off their roofs," I told him.

"If there's ever any rain," he said, "and there never is any."

"Or they can dig a well."

But he said they'd have to burrow clear to China.

But that's what people did on the mesa, dig wells, and I never heard of anybody coming up in China.

There was a pretty good old adobe up the side of a hill on the Colonias land, a nice big old house looking out at Taos Mountain across the valley. I decided to move in and add on. I made a big central fireplace in the living room and in general fixed it up into quite a nice home place. Then I cut up the rest of the Colonias land into one-acre pieces and started selling them off as subdivision lots. In a few years it was full of homes.

One day the president of the bank showed up in my office. "I understand you've got about $50,000 worth of paper," he said. "If you sold that, you'd have a good bit of money to invest. Maybe the bank would be interested in buying it from you."

I asked him, "How much would you want me to discount it?"

"Oh," he said, "maybe about forty percent."

I asked him, "Why would I want to sell it for sixty percent of its value when I own one hundred percent?"

Men sometimes think women are stupid.

Doris finally retired from teaching and came out west to live with me. I was very fond of Doris. She was good company, very intelligent and entertaining, and I was glad to have her.

In Taos back then everybody knew everybody. I knew Mabel Dodge and her Taos Indian husband Tony Lujan. Mabel took me around to her house several times and we got to be, if not friends, at least friendly acquaintances. And I knew Lady Dorothy Brett, who'd come to Taos with D. H. Lawrence and his wife Frieda. Lady Brett was English nobility and at first a little aloof, but then she decided I was OK and we got to be friends. She said her first date was with a young fellow named Winston Churchill. I knew Helene Wurlitzer, of the Wurlitzer Organ family, who started the Wurlitzer Foundation of Taos, which invites artists and writers to Taos to do their work at the Foundation, and I met Georgia O'Keeffe. Later on I sold Mabel Dodge's house to Dennis Hopper, who came into town a wild boy. A number of these people might have been famous, but they all just seemed like people to me.

I also knew Tinka Fechin. Her father Nikolai Fechin, a painter, had come to Taos in 1920, just before I first saw the place in my Model

T Ford. I knew Nola Karavas and her son Saki Karavas, who'd turned the old Columbian Hotel into La Fonda Hotel on the plaza. I knew Craig and Jenny Vincent. They lived in San Cristobal, a valley up toward Questa. They owned El Crepuscalo, the newspaper. I knew Spud Johnson, also a newspaperman.

So with Doris's help, I decided to throw a party and invite everybody I knew. I invited the artists, the writers, the whittlers and carvers, the ranchers, the businessmen, the Spanish farmers, and some Indian friends.

They all showed up, and they ate the food and drank the liquor, but they didn't party well together. They just seemed to fall into groups of people like themselves and not to mix. I found out that day that everybody's not like me. It never mattered to me who people were or what they did, I got along with them all.

The Spanish people owned the land in and around town where they had their little ranches, and the Taos Indians owned the best and prettiest land in Northern New Mexico, including the irrigated land up against the foothills and Taos Mountain itself. So as time passed I kept on investing in the only land available, the sagebrush land at the outskirts of Taos valley. Then I started selling it in one-acre plots.

First I developed Taos Mesa Estates, which in time became one of the nicer places to live in Taos. I sold the lots for $500. The last I heard, it was selling for about $25,000 an acre, if you can find anybody wants to sell.

My idea in real estate was to sell property at a reasonable price and make a little on it. Then when the new owner got around to selling it, he could make a little on it, too. And I let people pay the only way most of them could, on time. If anybody got behind on their payments, as people sometimes did if they were out of state or traveling, I let it slide or made the payments to the bank myself till I could locate them and give them a chance to catch up.

I always thought owning your own place was next to owning your own self. I never let anybody lose their land if I could help it.

I was living on the hill in Colonias, but I was still buying old places and renovating them when I discovered this big old adobe house of eleven rooms surrounded by cottonwoods on ten acres in Lower Ranchitos. It was a pretty place in the curve of the road with its own pastures and a stream running through and, down at the lower end, a little low cliff full of Indian rock carvings.

The place had gone through foreclosure seven years before, and the house had been very nearly demolished by vandals. The windows were all broken out, the plumbing had froze up, and the floors were rotten. You could take a douche in any room in the house if you turned on the pump, if you had a pump.

The roof was in bad repair. Apparently somebody had run out of money, so they'd put old linoleum rugs up there, even old burlap sacks, anything they could get hold of. It was really a mess. It was sagging and collecting water that had no way to drain, so leaks around the canales were so bad some of the adobe walls had melted back to dirt and straw and fallen into dirt mounds on the ground under them.

I bought the place and started working on the old house. For some time it was disintegrating around my ears, but that didn't kill me. Former tenants had left an old wood cook stove. If I got too cold I just stuck my feet in the oven and got warmed up and went back to work.

I had to take up the floors or else get my shins skinned every time I walked through the place. I tore up the old wood floors and filled in with gravel and poured in cement and then covered it with flagstone. You could get flagstone very reasonable from Las Vegas, New Mexico.

I had a Taos Indian man, Ventura Mirabal, working for me. Ventura could do anything. He'd been a bastard child, and he was a real loner. Now and then for a big job he hired some Indians he knew, but once he finished that job he fired them and went back to working alone. I trusted Ventura always knew what he was doing, and I let him alone to do it.

The Lower Ranchitos house was two-story, with one big long upstairs penthouse room. The place had been a lodge or road-house at one time, and the penthouse had been the dance floor. The vigas up there under that leaky roof were sagging badly in the middle.

Ventura put a beam the length of the room under the vigas and supported it with builder's jacks. Every few days he went up there and screwed the jacks up a half inch or so. Any faster and the vigas would have pulled out of the walls. Gradually Ventura raised the vigas into place with the beam under them, and the dip came out of the roof.

I could look down the old dug well in the yard and see it was full of trash. So I got a man in to clean it out. He was down there filling the bucket with all the old cans and rusted coat hangers and beat-up pails and junk, and I was hauling it up and emptying it.

When he finally got all the trash out, he yelled up, "There's a hell of a lot of worms in here."

He filled up the bucket with these great big night crawlers. When I saw that, I told him to come on up. Night crawlers are fine for fishing but not ideal for drinking water. So he stepped in the bucket and I pulled him out. We threw everything back in the well and I had a load of rocks dumped in it and sealed it up. We hauled water from town till I got a well drilled.

About a third of the ten acres was boggy and full of cattails, so I brought in a drag line from Alamosa. They dredged up the bog and got rid of the swamp with all those cattails. In its place I had two nice little lakes. I didn't have to leave home to go fishing anymore. I stocked the lakes with trout, and I had my fishing right at my back door. That was ideal for me. Above everything I loved to fish.

I'd already put the floor in the house, so I put the new plumbing outside the walls. The kibitzers in the neighborhood told me I had to dig down about four feet or the pipes would freeze. But I said, "No I won't. Just watch."

I dug ditches about two feet deep around the foundation, and walled and floored them with ninety-pound roll roofing. On top of that I put a layer of regular roll insulation, and in that I laid my pipes. Then with more insulation over them, and another layer of roll roofing on top, good roofing paper, I shoveled the dirt back in and covered the whole business up.

I never had a freeze-up in the plumbing, but the canales were another story. They kept freezing up on me. So I spread heat tapes all over the roof and into the canales. I hear they don't want you to do that anymore, but that was the last of my problem with frozen canales.

Slowly I got the place in shape. I built an extra room onto the house and put in a big fireplace. Once it was very comfortable and homelike, Doris and I moved in.

We both liked living there. Early in the morning and late in the day after I left the office, I could fish to my heart's content right at the time of day when they're biting.

I liked having animals around the place. I had my white Arabian stallion with me. He was pretty to see, out grazing in the pasture with magpies hitching a ride on his rump. One year a friend of mine dressed up in all the turquoise and silver I'd accumulated over the years and rode Shogy in the fiesta parade. Taos plaza had changed considerably since the day I first saw it in 1921 and drove people around it in the Model T who'd never seen a car before. Now it had cobbled pavement, and a landscaped center with a fountain.

Shogy was handsome with that big thick neck you get on stallions, and he showed off in the parade, side-stepping and prancing and performing for the crowd. Farmers around there started letting out their mares to accidentally get bred by the neighborhood stallion, and Shogy was happy to oblige. There got to be a lot of half-Arab horses in Lower Ranchitos.

Another pet animal was a calf I bought from an Indian out at Taos Pueblo. I named her Hildegarde, and I raised her myself on a bottle.

I must have fed her good because she got to be enormous. About the same time, I got a sheep and named him Oswald. Oswald and Hildegarde got to be inseparable pals.

Once a year Oswald had to be sheared. When the shearers came around, I had to separate the buddies because Hildegarde thought they were killing Oswald. She bellowed and kicked the corral fence and carried on, and one year, like the cow that jumped over the moon, she sailed over the fence and lit into the shearers to save Oswald from this terrible fate.

When Hildegarde got herself bred and had a baby, Oswald protected the calf like he thought he was the daddy. I named the calf Esmeralda. Hildegarde had the biggest udder I ever saw. I had to apply udder balm daily to keep her comfortable so Esmeralda could nurse.

I couldn't let all that lush pasture go to waste, so I bought a few Black Angus. When it came time for one of the heifers to deliver, she couldn't drop her calf. I saw it was going to be a breech birth. So I had to go in again, like I'd had to now and then on the ranch, and turn the calf around so it could come out head first. After that, mother and son prospered.

I fed a host of stray cats that turned up on the place. Of course they multiplied, so eventually I thought I'd better catch a few and take them to the shelter. So I put out a trap.

Instead of cats I caught a baby skunk. I covered the trap with a big flower pot so the skunk couldn't spray me, then opened the trap and let it out. It never sprayed me at all. I think it knew I was doing it a favor. It's terrible the way people de-scent pet skunks. Without the scent glands, they're very vulnerable. That spray is their only defense.

It was a good life in Lower Ranchitos. I had everything just the way I wanted it, except the hill across the road presented a nuisance. It was a dirt bikers' playground, a lovers' lane, and a garbage dump conveniently rolled into one. When I got tired of the annoyance I bought the hill. But I had no use for it myself. So I had Joe Duran bring in his heavy equipment and clean up the garbage and scrape in roads. Then just as I'd done with Colonias and Taos Mesa Estates, I cut it into building sites and sold it off. Now it's full of nice homes. It was called Blueberry Hill. I understand the name has spread to cover most of the lower end of the mesa.

A little later on, I went in with a couple of partners, the Bowers from Silver City—Kathy was head of the English Department at the college there—and we developed a big piece of sage and piñon land out on the edge of the Rio Grande Gorge, above the John Dunne bridge. We called it *Tierra de los Rios.*

We sold it in ten-acre plots for $500 an acre, on time so people could afford it. A lot of people out there built their homes themselves. Now it's worth five or ten thousand an acre. It has lots of large piñon trees and good views of the mountains and, just down the hill, Hondo Valley that runs to the river with its hot springs. It's quiet, peaceful country.

My sister Doris was diabetic, but she loved sweets and, for all I could do, hid them everywhere in the house. I was gone most of the time, in the office or showing property, so I couldn't always be watching out for her.

We'd kept up with each other since I was just a little kid—all through my days at H. J. Heinz and Westinghouse, through that terrible marriage to the preacher and lighting out for New Mexico in the Model T with a nine-months-old baby in a basket on the seat beside me, all through my struggles in Albuquerque and my adventures on the ranches—almost my whole life. In the summers, she visited me on the ranches and later at the lodge in Datil, and then came to live with me once she retired from teaching. We'd kept up with each other and been friends since childhood. Doris was the best friend I ever had.

Well, in the late 1960s Doris had an insulin attack and died. Her death was a terrible blow. So now I was living alone. I saw I had no need of that big house, so I cut it up into four apartments and rented them out, and I cleaned out a little cabin for myself down a bit lower on the property. At one time it had been a chicken house. So it was my second chicken-house home, my first one back during my days in Albuquerque. It was very livable. It was right across from one of the fishing ponds. In time I added an upstairs, just one big room with views.

23 | MY CIRCLE EXPANDS

Along in the early '70s a singer and actress, Janice Mars, came to Taos from New York City because she liked Frank Waters's books and set out to meet him. Well, she fell in love with Taos and decided to buy a piece of land. So Frank brought her into my office and I sold her a piece of land out on Taos Mesa.

After she went back to New York, Janice kept in touch. She was fed up with life in the big city, so eventually she came back to Taos and went to work for me in the office.

Janice wanted to know all about everything. She was forever asking me questions. An animal lover, she asked me one day how I felt about my cows going to slaughter. I tried to skirt around that by saying my cows went to feed lots. But she wouldn't let me off the hook. She told me I knew where they eventually ended up. So I just told her we all have our fate, and that was a cow's.

Janice could type and do letters and business papers, and that was real helpful. I'd been hiring out that kind of work. And she turned out to be a good real estate salesman. She soon got her license, and she sold a lot of land to friends of hers visiting from both coasts—actors and actresses and singers. Marlon Brando came out several times. They'd been in some actors' studio together in New York City when they were young, Janice and Marlon and Maureen Stapleton and Kim Stanley and Marilyn Monroe. Some of them—Maureen and her two children—stayed at the big house on Lower Ranchitos whenever they came out to Taos. Kim lived there in one of the apartments for a time. And Marlon visited and looked at land around Taos and in other parts of the state.

One night a bunch of us went to Albuquerque in a Dodge RV I'd taken in on a piece of land. We were going to see Kim in *Streetcar Named Desire.* After the play, Marlon wanted to take over the driving and do a little sight-seeing, though it was very late. He drove over every curb on Santa Fe plaza on our way home. He was the worst driver I ever saw in my life.

One time when he wanted to go land-hunting, Janice drove down to the Albuquerque airport the night before and slept in her truck with her two Weimaraners so they could get an early start as soon as he got off the plane.

Marlon and Janice were old friends, but they couldn't get along peaceably for two days set end to end. The arguments started as soon as he got off the plane, and they continued all up and down and around the southern part of New Mexico till Janice just turned around and put him back on a plane to LA.

He never bought any land out here, except for a little piece in Ruidoso, but he'd taken a liking to my Dodge RV, the one he drove over all the curbs on Santa Fe plaza. One time when he was out here he talked me into selling it to him. He drove it back to LA and ended up giving it to a leader in the American Indian Movement. It was later found all shot up to hell and gone some place in Oregon.

Pretty soon I had the FBI show up in Taos to question me. They'd been flying around in helicopters, keeping an eye on that Dodge RV. Turned out it was still in my name. Marlon had never changed the registration. Here I was in my seventies with the FBI wanting to know what I was doing running around Oregon in an RV with these Indian revolutionaries. I told the agents I hadn't been up there but

I sure wished I had. I had to take them to the bank and prove I'd sold the camper to Marlon. I guess after that Marlon himself had a visit from the Feds.

Sometime in the late sixties two smart fellows came through Taos— I don't know where they were from—and figured out a clever way to make money. They bought up a twelve-hundred-acre sheep ranch across the Rio Grande Gorge from Taos for $12 an acre. They divided it up into one-acre plots and scraped some roads through the sage and put up street signs. Then they went to the Seattle World's Fair and got themselves a booth and put up a sign said WIN AN ACRE HOME SITE WITH GORGEOUS VIEWS JUST OUTSIDE OF BEAUTIFUL TAOS NEW MEXICO, or to that effect.

Lots of people filled out a slip with their name and address and dropped it in the box. Imagine their surprise when every last one of them found out they were winners. They'd won themselves a gorgeous acre lot outside of beautiful Taos, New Mexico. All they had to do was pay 'closing costs' of $250 or thereabouts. These two guys made $250 an acre on land they'd bought for $12 an acre. That was a pretty good return on their money.

People started coming into my office asking for directions to their beautiful one-acre home sites. Pretty soon I found out where the acres were. When I went out there, the desert wind had blown down the signs, the sage was coming back, and you could barely make out the roads.

That land was suitable for sheep—ranchers could put in stock tanks and haul water out to them—but it wasn't suitable for people. When they showed up in Taos looking for their land, I told them they'd have to dig till they hit the Yalu River before they'd find any water out there in that sage desert. They left my office pretty disgusted. I understand those two fellows that sold it for 'closing costs' got caught for the swindle and spent time in jail.

A summer or so later a salmon fisherman from Seattle came through

Taos and stopped by the office wanting to know how to get to the beautiful one-acre plot he'd won at the Seattle World's Fair. When I told him the story, he took it real well, had a good laugh out of it. I let him know I envied him making a living out of fishing. He told me to get rid of that acre for him for anything I could get out of it and he'd take me salmon fishing in Seattle.

After a little while a fellow came along wanting to buy a piece of land for next to nothing, so I took him out to see the salmon fisherman's acre. The land out there did have beautiful views, that part of the story was true. Turned out it was just what this fellow wanted. He planned to put a small trailer on it to have a hideaway for meditation. Maybe he was a hippie, I don't know. We had a number of people meditating around Taos about then. Anyway, I sold it to him and sent whatever I got for it to the salmon fisherman in Seattle.

I heard back from him right away. He'd got a kick out of the whole deal and he invited me out to Washington State to go fishing with him. So Janice and I got in my Volkswagen camper and headed northwest, sight-seeing and camping along the way.

We had the time of our lives in Washington. We brought little individual cans of salmon back with us to Taos and made presents of them to all our friends and customers. Everybody thought we'd caught the salmon ourselves, and we didn't disabuse them of the notion. But actually it rained every day we were in Seattle and the water was so rough we never got to do any fishing. We did get a kick out of spending time in the man's cannery, though, canning salmon ourselves. That part of our yarn was true.

It looks like in my later years I've gotten to know a lot of artists of one kind or another. Along with all the actors from New York and Hollywood, as time went on I got to know a number of artists and writers who came to the Wurlitzer Foundation. Some bought land from me and stayed in Taos and made it their home. I was always looking for fishing buddies, so I often invited a few of them on all-day fishing trips in my Volkswagen Camper. They called it my Hippiemobile.

They were considerably younger than me. As I get older I seem to draw young people around me. It feels natural. I've never got the hang of being old. Maybe they think I'm a character. Maybe I am. These Wurlitzer people liked hearing stories from my life, or they were polite enough to let me think so.

I'd get up before daybreak and barbecue ribs and make potato salad, and I was ready to go when they turned up half-asleep at five A.M. By sunup we were heading out across the mesa and down the gorge to the Rio Grande, or northwest for Hopewell Lake, or for Lagunitas up by the Brazos.

We fished all morning, stopped to eat our picnic lunch, then fished all afternoon. I chum a little with salmon eggs or corn, and I usually caught a string of bass or trout. Sometimes the artists caught some too.

After sunset, along about twilight, we'd pack up and head back to Taos. We sang all the way home, blues songs I remembered from my days with Monty Blue and his orchestra, or spirituals I learned as a kid in the tobacco barns down in Virginia. I still had a voice and I always sang my favorite:

> With someone like you, a pal good and true,
> I'd like to leave it all behind and go and find,
> A place that's known to God alone,
> Just a spot to call our own.
> I'll build a little nest,
> Somewhere out in the West
> And let the rest of the world go by.

Whoever wrote that song expressed my life. One time I asked Janice if she thought I could have been a singer on the stage. She said I could've sung with Eddie Cantor and The Ziegfeld Follies. Maybe she was just saying that, I don't know.

Some of those writers and artists were fishermen, but most were city kids. So once they caught their fish I'd say, "Now I guess you want me to gut them for you," and they'd allow as how they did. Then I'd say, "And I guess you want me to scale them for you," and they'd say they wouldn't mind. And once back at my place I'd say, "I guess you want me to cook them up for you." They were always glad to stay for dinner.

I've liked having all those people around—the actors and singers and painters and writers. One fellow's an opera singer. When he comes for a visit, I make him do his practicing in another part of the house. I'm still not crazy about anything classical—it's blues and gospel for me. A lot of people bore me, though I try not to show it, but these artist types never do. They entertain me, and I give them practical advice. I guess it's a fair exchange. I'd have liked to do something like they do myself, but I had to make a living.

In '76 I think it was, a doctor and his wife came along who wanted the Lower Ranchitos place with the house and two ponds worse than I did, so I sold it to them. I'd turned it into quite a picturesque place, one of the nicer places in Taos, with beautiful great big willows and cottonwood trees and those two trout ponds and the stream cutting through the pastures. A little way down from the house, at the little bluff along the stream, Indians in the old days had scratched a lot of pictures in the rock there. People were always wanting a look at them. You could make out stick men and a snake or two, but other drawings were mysteries.

I had to have a place to live, so I bought a piece of property out on South Santa Fe Highway about two miles out of Taos. Except for the Ford dealership, there was nobody out there at all at that time. I built a log house to live in and a three-car garage and a log office building. Now I understand it's a strip development out there, jam-full of motels and businesses that dwarf my little log spread. I guess I started all that. At the time nobody thought of building that far out of town. I expect a lot of people wish it'd never occurred to me, either.

But now I had my real estate business right at home instead of having to go into town. I was getting up in my seventies, and it was convenient to be able to take off work and go in the house and fix lunch but still see any customers who drove up.

People buying desert real estate were naturally worried about having enough water. So to show people how to survive in a desert, I collected rainwater off the roofs of all three buildings and funneled it through a filter—a garbage can filled with charcoal—into a clean new septic-tank cistern sunk in the ground. Wherever I lived I liked to grow my own food, so I always had a garden. On South Santa Fe Road I collected enough water off the roofs to water a half-acre garden out back of the house. Sometimes I had so much water I had to empty the tank, just let the water run on off.

When next Marlon came out, he brought with him a beautiful young woman named Jill who later returned to Taos and went to work for me along with Janice in the office. I was very fond of Jill. After a year or so her mother got sick, and she had to return to Los Angeles to take care of her.

Jill was killed out there when a semi pulling two trailers hooked into her little car and dragged it. That was a real shame. They never did anything to that truck driver, just called it an accident. I call it negligence.

By this time I had developed seven subdivisions on the sage land around Taos—Taos Mesa Estates, *Las Colonias, Tierra de los Rios,* Blueberry Hill, and several others. I was doing very well in Taos until I got arthritis in my lower extremities. Friends tried everything they could think of for the pain—even melting paraffin and mixing it with mineral oil and putting it around my knees where it turned into a soft warm waxy wrap. As the pain got worse I decided I'd better move to a warmer climate. By this time I was getting close to eighty years old. So I moved to T or C.

Somebody ought to hang old Ralph Edwards for getting the town's name changed to Truth or Consequences. The people there seem to think it's all right, but I wouldn't have my mail sent to any place with a name like that. I bought a place in Williamsburg, a small settlement just a little way south. The proper name for the town, the name it had been called for many years, was Hot Springs because it was a health spa. Now people don't even know that it was originally Hot Springs, New Mexico. However, that's neither here nor there. I can't run the world so I don't need to worry about it.

I bought a house on the hill across the road from the river running down from Elephant Butte dam. I wanted to be on the hill because that's an old dam and it holds a lot of water. I wondered how sound it is. I moved there to see if the hot springs would help my arthritis. By this time I was having a lot of pain.

I would like to know, since we're on the subject, why all the adver-tisements call it "minor arthritis pains." Anybody that has it knows there's nothing minor about it. It's major. I can tell you because I've had it in my knees for the last fifteen years. You go in to see a doc-tor and ask him for help, and he doesn't tell you anything, just gives you a couple of pills and sends you home fifty bucks poorer.

I stayed in T or C a few years. I had Janice and my daughter Anita, who was widowed by then, living on the hill with me, Anita in the house and Janice in a cabin I built on the place. And though I was crippled up I went on dabbling in real estate. Like me, other old peo-ple came there to retire on account of the baths, but when one half of a couple died the other half usually wanted to move back closer to the kids. At that point they were eager to sell out, so I'd buy up the house for their equity, maybe a little more, and have repairs done if they were needed, and then sell and hold the mortgage on the prop-erty. That way I made the interest. I'd begun putting together a trust fund for Anita and my grandchildren, something for them to count on when I was gone. I was responsible for them being in the world, wasn't I?

After a few years I saw the baths weren't doing anything for me, and I decided once again to move on. I was way up in my eighties by then and I knew this would be my last move. I looked around Santa Fe, but there were too many restrictions about what you could do with your own property. I finally settled in Silver City. Silver was familiar to me. I'd been in and out of there when I had the ranches or when I was haul-ing cattle or horses or feed in my two big semi trucks.

After I left T or C the people there got all excited when Ted Turner and his wife Jane Fonda bought a big piece of land somewhere around Reserve. There were rumors going that Jane Fonda was going to start up one of her exercise parlors in T or C to go with the baths, and T or C would get rejuvenated into a great big world-famous health resort. People will believe anything.

Anyway, I bought this house on Little Walnut Road in Silver City that I'm living in today. It's big enough for each of us—Anita and

Janice and me—to have our own space, and I'm sitting here in front of the fire to tell my tale.

If I can talk somebody—like my friend the mayor Dan Dunegan—into looking at a property for me, I still dabble in real estate. And old friends come down from Taos—a couple of the writers I used to take fishing with me, a painter, a hotel owner from up in the ski valley that I helped finance in the start of his hotel business, and the opera singer from Tucson. If he decides he has to practice while he's here, I make him sing songs I like, none of that grand opera business.

A few old friends are left in Silver, like Kathy Bower. She and her husband were my old partners in the development of *Tierra de los Rios* up in Taos. My stepdaughter Dorothy comes through from Denver a couple time a year in her big RV, and my granddaughters visit—Kryssi Peterson from Pine Bluffs, Wyoming, and Ann Mary Ozlear from Sewickley, Pennsylvania, and Sarah Peck from the Big Island of Hawaii.

Once while Sarah was here some friends of hers from Hawaii came through in an RV the fellow had converted from a Greyhound bus. In my day, in addition to that first Model T, I've had truck campers, a VW camper, an Airstream trailer, and that Dodge RV Marlon talked me out of, but I never saw such luxury on wheels as that converted Greyhound bus.

He told me people keep asking him how he gets that thing to the mainland from Hawaii and he tells them he just drives it through the tunnel. They just nod and say "Oh" like they're embarrassed they hadn't figured that out for themselves. I got a kick out of that. Nobody ever likes to admit to ignorance.

Well, Doris is dead, and Hildegarde and Esmeralda, and some bastard shot Oswald right in my own pasture. Shogy died and is buried in my garden on South Santa Fe Road in Taos. The old dog has died, and so has Dick, my cat, who always slept with me with his head on the other pillow, stretched out just like me, I've got photos to prove it. I almost died myself several years ago when a polyp burst in my intestines. I was rushed to the hospital bleeding so bad it looked like nothing they did was going to stop it. They'd about given me up. I was on my way out.

Then while my body was lying in the hospital bed, I found myself walking over the Gila mountains, taking great huge loping steps in slow motion like the men on the moon, and at my side was Jesus. He has always been my friend. It was such a beautiful experience I was saddened when all of a sudden he stopped and told me I had to go back, it wasn't yet my time. I was sorry he'd changed his mind.

I was disappointed to find myself back in that hospital bed. As a last resort the doctor had given me a saline enema, and that had stopped the bleeding. The doctor told me I had diverticulitis from eating so much New Mexico chili, and it's true I've always loved it, the hotter the better.

The Good Book says there's a season for everything, one for planting, one for harvest, one for birth and another for dying. I was ninety-two years old. I thought it was my time and I was ready. But here I am, back again. It'll all be to do over one day.

I'd like to make it to a hundred. I'm in a race with George Burns, a race where the winner comes in last. But however much longer I'm around, I think Jesus will be with me on that journey we've still got to finish. Whatever mischief I've done is done already, at my age I won't be doing any more. So I doubt it'll be to the bad place because Jesus wouldn't be the one guiding me there.

People stop by and I enjoy having them, and people from Taos come to visit. I can't cook for them like I used to, they have to look after themselves. And people send me jokes in the mail because they know I like to laugh. Of course I have to wait till somebody will read them to me because I can't see worth a durn any more. When I'm alone, to keep my brain working I make up jokes and riddles in my head and then bore anybody willing to listen to them.

The other day my doctor came by to show me her new baby, and my visiting nurse practitioner comes every week and tells me all about her horse and the country where she rides. And my friend

Dan Dunegan—he's the mayor and a realtor, too—stops in and tells me about properties for sale. Sometimes I buy up a place and turn it over, just to keep my hand in.

Rosa Acuna comes around whenever I need her help—Rosa can do anything—and Janice helps me run this machine so I can tell my tale. My fingers have got too clumsy to push the buttons even if I could see the buttons and read the labels saying what the buttons are for.

I've no complaints. I've had a good life. I've enjoyed it. I can't get around much anymore. First I walked with a cane, then with two, and now with a walker. It's my off-road vehicle. I can see well enough to know when a car runs up the driveway, but not good enough to tell who it is, or to look at television, though I listen to the news— the local, not the national, I can't do anything about that.

I've worked hard all my life, but work's always been my pleasure. I'd tell myself in the morning: get up and do something even if it's wrong; do the best you can with the tools you've got; if you're not making mistakes you're not doing anything. I can still recite every last verse of "The Ride of Jenny McNeal" for anybody fool enough to listen, and I can sit here enjoying the fire. I have one every day all winter long and sometimes into the summer, too, because even in warm weather I sometimes get chilly. A fire is just so comfortable. It's a whole hell of a lot of company. I can feel the heat and see the glow and hear it cackling back at me.

Preparing Frances Minerva Nunnery's life story for publication, I began to detect a number of themes that ran through it like subliminal tracings. What called itself to my attention was the similarity of her story to women's lives from as far back as pre-Revolutionary War journals and continuing through the journals of pioneer women. These tell us what ills women experienced. Perhaps a woman could not feed her children, or perhaps she lost her home when her husband died or even, in one case, went to jail. Likewise when good things happened—a recovery from illness, a marriage, childbirth—we're usually told only that it happened, hardly ever how the woman felt about it.

On the journey west in covered wagons, women's diaries and journals tell of fending off Indian attacks, of mules or oxen swept away in a river crossing, of treasured household goods—a bedstead, a chiffonier, a rocking chair or pie chest—abandoned to lighten the animals' load, or of a child dying along the trail and left in a scratched-out grave. The most we can do is guess what the woman felt when grandma's rocker had to be left along the trail, or when the little one who "had a sweet look about him . . . couldn't nurse and lasted only a fortnight." One woman writes that she was "some months pregnant but her husband Matthew was in a lather to go." We hear of Matthew's "lather" but nothing of her terror of heading pregnant into the unknown in an ox-drawn wagon without springs.

Similarly, as Frances tells her life story she says little about her feelings. We learn all about what she did but not necessarily how she felt. We do hear early that she "felt like an orphan," but also that she was proud to be her mother's daughter, and later that she "couldn't stand" the man her mother made her marry. She tells us that her mother was a remarkable woman, that Amelia Jane Hill, twice and perhaps thrice married, "could do anything," and we discover as we read that Frances certainly took after Amelia Jane in that. Frances never passes judgment on her mother for favoring sister Irene, for taking all the wages Frances earned from the time she was a child of thirteen to pay off the mortgage on the farm, for marrying her off at age twenty to a man she had seen only once and came to hate for what sounds like marital rape and continued sexual abuse in the name of a husband's "rights." We do learn that when her mother disapproved of the divorce because "we never had a divorce in this family," Frances stood up for herself: "Yes," she said, "but you don't have to live with him." We don't know how she felt when she learned of her mother's further betrayal: keeping in touch with the hated husband and telling him where Anita was, enabling him to kidnap the child and take her out of the country. And we can but guess how she felt when her beloved ranches were sold, though she does tell us that the winters alone on Spur Ranch and Centerfire were the happiest times of her life.

We learn who Frances was from what she did. Like the pioneer women, she was nothing if not a survivor, and like her mother she could do anything. Her success was based on her willingness to undertake any job and, if it didn't work out to suit her, to try something else. We learn of her strength and self-sufficiency from the story of her horse's slip on ice that landed horse and rider at the bottom of a rocky canyon, when she mounted again sore and bleeding and rode four miles back home, got in her truck, and drove to the hospital in Springerville where she had to stay for some days, or from the story of her careening ride down Salt River Canyon with a truckload of horses after her air brakes popped, and at the bottom getting out, reconnecting the air brakes, and driving on into Phoenix.

Though twice married, she spent most of her life alone but for the friends, younger and younger as she got older, who were drawn to her stories and her willingness to listen to troubles and give practical advice, and who looked forward to the daylong fishing outings at a mountain lake, and the drives home in her VW camper singing along with her still remarkable voice all of her favorite hymns and blues songs from her youth.

Frances was born with the twentieth century and she died with it. She adapted readily to all the changes it brought, from horse and buggy to rockets to the moon, but I doubt she enjoyed the transformation of farming and ranching into agribusiness, of Taos into a tourist attraction, or of large stretches of her beloved New Mexico into the homes of weapons-makers and nuclear waste.

Her time has come and gone, and Frances with it. But we live it all again as we read her remarkable life story as she alone could tell it.